Best Easy Day Hikes Series

Best Easy Day Hikes

National Park

Fourth Edition

Ron Adkison and Ben Adkison

FALCONGUIDES

GUILFORD, CONNECTICUT
HELENA, MONTANA

DAVIE COUNTY PUBLIC LIBRARY
MOCKSVILLE, NORTH CAROLINA

FALCONGUIDES®

An imprint of Rowman & Littlefield
Falcon, FalconGuides, and Outfit Your Mind are registered trademarks of Rowman & Littlefield.

Distributed by NATIONAL BOOK NETWORK

Copyright © 2017 by Rowman & Littlefield

Maps © Rowman & Littlefield

All rights reserved. No part of this book may be reproduced in any form or by any electronic or mechanical means, including information storage and retrieval systems, without written permission from the publisher, except by a reviewer who may quote passages in a review.

British Library Cataloguing-in-Publication Information available

Library of Congress Cataloging-in-Publication Data available

ISBN 978-1-4930-2298-4 (paperback)
ISBN 978-1-4930-2299-1 (e-book)

♾™ The paper used in this publication meets the minimum requirements of American National Standard for Information Sciences—Permanence of Paper for Printed Library Materials, ANSI/NISO Z39.48-1992.

The authors and Rowman & Littlefield assume no liability for accidents happening to, or injuries sustained by, readers who engage in the activities described in this book.

Contents

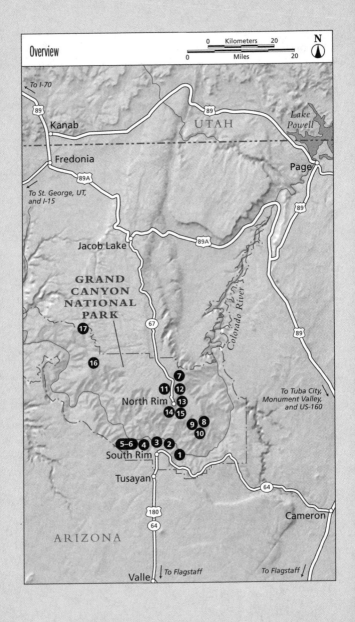

Acknowledgments

Although changes to the landscapes of the Grand Canyon of the Colorado River (the Big Ditch) are almost imperceptible in our lifetimes, the complexities of land (and people) management in Grand Canyon National Park are in a constant state of evolution. Keeping a hiking guide to Grand Canyon National Park up to date is a never-ending process; and for me, it's a labor of love.

Once again, I offer my humble and grateful thanks to those who were so generous with their advice, expertise, guidance, and wisdom in the previous editions of this book: John Rihs, Andy Thorstenson, Bil Vandergraff, Bryan Wisher, Steve Sullivan, and Helen Fairly.

Many management decisions that affect visitors have taken place since the first edition of this book was published in 1998, particularly on the South Rim. Todd R. Berger, managing editor of the Grand Canyon Association, and Judy Hellmich, chief of interpretation at Grand Canyon National Park, offered invaluable assistance and guidance during the update of this edition. Thank you.

Last but certainly not least, my wife and best friend, Nancy, provided me with the support and inspiration to make the fourth edition of *Best Easy Day Hikes Grand Canyon National Park* possible.

—Ron Adkison

Map Legend

89	US Highway
64	State Highway
	Local Road
= = = = = =	Unpaved Road
▬▬▬▬▬▬	Featured Trail
- - - - - - -	Trail
├─┼─┼─┼─┤	Railroad
~~	River/Creek
—·—·—	Intermittent River/Creek
⌢⌢⌢⌢	Cliff
	National Forest
	Local/State Park
▲	Backcountry Campsite
⏝	Bridge
Δ	Camping
∩	Cavern/Cave/Natural Bridge
┇	Gate
P	Parking
⏓	Pass/Gap
▲	Peak
⊞	Picnic Area
■	Point of Interest/Structure
⛺	Ranger Station
∥	Rapids
⛨	Restroom
⟋	Spring
☎	Telephone
○	Town
⓫	Trailhead
◉	Viewpoint/Overlook
❓	Visitor/Information Center

Introduction

Although thousands of backpackers flock to Grand Canyon National Park each year, many more thousands of visitors don't have the time or desire to undertake a multiday backpack trip below the canyon rim. Luckily, the park offers many excellent day hiking opportunities, and some of the park trails are suitable for novice hikers, even families with small children. Unlike backpacking in the Grand Canyon, day hiking is free and requires no permits.

This indispensable guide to the Canyon's best easy day hikes is an abridged version of the comprehensive *Hiking Grand Canyon National Park* (FalconGuides). It is the only book dedicated exclusively to day hiking trails in the Grand Canyon. For visitors on a tight schedule or anyone wishing to take a short walk on the park's excellent trails, this book allows readers to quickly and easily choose hikes best suited to their abilities, goals, and time constraints.

The seventeen day hikes described in this book range in length from less than 1 mile to nearly 12 miles long, although most hikes average between 2 and 3 miles. Most hikes follow plateau-top trails with minimal elevation gain and loss. Also included are longer plateau-top day hikes that will satisfy more serious hikers who are budgeting time and energy. Since no book of day hikes in the Grand Canyon would be complete without a few hikes below the canyon rim, some of the "easier" Inner Canyon day hikes are included here for energetic and fit hikers who wish to sample the Canyon's inner depths. Almost all of the hikes in this book are round-trip hikes, tracing well-defined trails that are easy to follow. Most of these trails lead to dramatic vista points.

Hikers should bear in mind that hiking anywhere in Grand Canyon National Park can be challenging. All hikes begin at moderately high elevations, ranging from 6,600 to 8,800 feet. Hikers not acclimated to high elevations should take it easy for a few days before tackling a trail leading below the rim. Hikes below the rim, even those of short distance, can be very difficult for hikers unused to the rigors of Grand Canyon hiking.

For more information about Grand Canyon National Park and its network of trails, contact:

Grand Canyon National Park
P.O. Box 129
Grand Canyon, AZ 86023
(928) 638-7888
www.nps.gov/grca

Maps

A variety of good maps show the trails of Grand Canyon National Park, and I recommend two for users of this book.

The first is the *Trails Illustrated Grand Canyon National Park* topographic map, which shows all the trails in the park, many beyond the scope of this book, from River Mile 42 to River Mile 139 near Deer Creek in the central Grand Canyon. Trails Illustrated maps are available at many stores and gas stations in communities adjacent to the park; at the visitor center at Canyon View Information Plaza; at Market Plaza on the South Rim; at the General Store on the North Rim; and at the North Rim Country Store on the Kaibab Plateau. To order Trails Illustrated maps from the Grand Canyon Association, call (928) 638-2481 or visit www.grandcanyon.org.

The second map I recommend is particularly useful for navigating forest roads on the Kaibab Plateau. It is the *North*

Kaibab District Map of the Kaibab National Forest. You can get Kaibab National Forest maps at the Tusayan Ranger Station, a short distance north of the town of Tusayan; near the south entrance to the park; at the North Kaibab Ranger Station in Fredonia; and at the Kaibab Plateau Visitor Center at Jacob Lake.

The US Geological Survey (USGS) and Earthwalk Press also put out good maps of the Canyon area. These maps are available at Market Plaza and many gift shops on the South Rim.

Zero Impact

The desert landscape of the Grand Canyon appears deceptively durable. Actually it is very fragile. Once damaged, the desert recovers slowly and may not heal completely in your lifetime, if at all. Soils in the Grand Canyon are thin to nonexistent, and plants and desert creatures have evolved a delicate balance of survival. The simple acts of walking off the trail (even for a short distance), crushing plants, or moving rocks disrupt the balance that desert plants and animals have achieved. Taking shortcuts and excavating earth at campsites hasten erosion of the thin soil cover, reducing and, in some instances, eliminating habitat. Shortcutting trails can lead to the eventual destruction of a good (perhaps unmaintained) trail.

Most Grand Canyon hikers have long since learned to employ zero-impact practices. Along most of the Canyon's trails you seldom will find trash, food scraps, or discarded items. Happily, hikers rarely leave soapsuds in precious water sources, evidence of illegal campfires, or signs of unnecessary excavations or alterations. If you wish to be environmentally sensitive, consider the following ideas for zero-impact travel as guidelines for preserving the wilderness resource—not only for the Canyon's native inhabitants but also for those who follow in your footsteps.

Manage Camp Waste

Garbage and food scraps attract animals and insects. Pack out your garbage and leftover food scraps with the rest of your trash.

Deposit human waste at least 200 feet from campsites, trails, water sources, and drainages. Choose a spot with organic soil and dig a cat hole 6 to 8 inches deep, covering the waste with soil. Do not bury or burn your toilet paper. Fires from burning toilet paper have devastated parts of the Canyon; Deer Creek and Hance Creek are examples. You must pack out all used toilet paper in the Grand Canyon. Resealable plastic bags are useful for this.

Three Falcon Principles of Zero Impact

- Leave with everything you brought.
- Leave no sign of your visit.
- Leave the landscape as you found it.

Stay on the Trail

The passage of too many feet creates a lasting trail in the Grand Canyon desert, whether it be from campsite to water source or an off-trail route that can evolve into a trail. Use established trails where they are available. Your boot tracks in trail-less areas will encourage others to follow. Walk on rock surfaces whenever possible.

Avoid Biological Soil Crust

In some areas of the Grand Canyon you will find large areas of soil covered by a black or gray lumpy crust, also called cryptobiotic soil crust. This crust is a delicate assemblage of mosses, lichens, blue-green algae, and fungi forming a protective layer against wind and water erosion. The crust aids in the soil's absorption and retention of moisture, allowing larger plants to gain a foothold. The passage of a single hiker can destroy this fragile crust, which may take twenty-five years or longer to redevelop. In areas covered by biological soil crust, hikers must stick to established trails.

Respect Archaeological and Historical Sites

Evidence of ancient cultures and prospectors-turned-tour guides abounds on Grand Canyon trails. Indeed, all Inner Canyon trails except the South Kaibab Trail have evolved from routes used by ancient inhabitants that were later improved upon by nineteenth-century prospectors. Along some trails you may encounter archaeological and historical ruins and artifacts. Granaries, rock art, ruins of dwellings, potsherds, the gray ash and charcoal of mescal roasting pits, prospectors' cabins, and mining and camp relics are among the cultural resources hikers may find in the Grand Canyon backcountry.

The majority of archaeological sites date back to between a.d. 1050 and a.d. 1200, a time when the Ancestral Puebloan people widely occupied the Grand Canyon region. Ancient granaries and ruins are very fragile, so restrain the urge to enter them and climb on their stone walls. Walk carefully around the slopes that support these structures. Ruins may be the highlight of a hike, but they are inappropriate places to camp or eat meals. Food crumbs and garbage may attract rodents that could then nest in the site and damage it.

Pigments of ancient pictographs are easily destroyed by skin oils. Restrain the urge to touch them, particularly handprint pictographs. Never add your own graffiti to irreplaceable rock writing panels. If you happen upon an archaeological site where artifacts remain, you may photograph them, but if you pick up or rearrange objects, you may be destroying an important link to the past. Once an artifact is removed or disturbed, it becomes merely an object with little meaning to archaeologists.

Keep in mind that these nonrenewable resources offer archaeologists insights into past ways of life in the Grand Canyon and can be easily disturbed and damaged by curious hikers. Although federal and state laws protect cultural resources, ultimately it depends on each of us to walk softly and treat these resources with the respect they deserve. Excavation and stabilization of many sites have yet to take place. Although you are likely to encounter many such sites on Grand Canyon trails, this book will not lead you to them, preserving for hikers the sense of discovery.

Shuttle Services

Four free shuttle bus routes on the South Rim provide access to all trailheads between Yaki Point in the east to Hermits Rest in the west. Tickets are not required (the Tusayan Shuttle requires a park pass), and all bus stops are clearly marked with signs. Departure times vary greatly depending upon season. Times below are for the summer season. Please be at the shuttle stop 30 minutes before the last shuttle of the day. Consult the *Guide,* the park's information newspaper, or visit Grand Canyon National Park's Web site at www.nps .gov/grca. A North Rim shuttle is available to hikers for a small fee.

Hermits Rest Route Shuttle

Hermit Road is closed to private vehicles to relieve congestion from March 1 through November 30. During that time, the Hermits Rest Shuttle operates daily, running every fifteen to thirty minutes from 4:00 a.m. to one hour after sunset. There is no fee. You can board the bus at the Village Route Transfer bus stop, adjacent to Bright Angel Lodge and the Bright Angel trailhead. This shuttle is useful for hikers going to the Rim Trail, Hermits Rest to Santa Maria Spring, and Hermits Rest to Dripping Springs (Hikes 4, 5, and 6).

Kaibab Trail Route Shuttle

The Kaibab Trail Route Shuttle connects the Canyon View Information Plaza area with the South Kaibab trailhead and Yaki Point. The shuttle operates daily, running every fifteen to thirty minutes from 4:30 a.m. to one hour after sunset.

The Hiker's Express Shuttle takes an early-morning route from Bright Angel Lodge to the Backcountry Information Center, Grand Canyon Visitor Center, and on to the South Kaibab trailhead. The Hiker's Express operates May through September and leaves the Bright Angel Lodge on the hour 4:00 to 7:00 a.m. These two shuttles serve hikers taking the South Kaibab Trail to Cedar Ridge (Hike 2).

Village Route Shuttle

The Village Route Shuttle connects the Hermits Rest Route to the Kaibab Trail Route. The shuttle makes stops at all the hotels, restaurants, campgrounds, and other services in the village and Market Plaza area. It operates daily, running every fifteen to thirty minutes from 4:00 a.m. to 11:00 p.m.

Tusayan Shuttle

The project was started in conjunction with plans for creating more parking within Tusayan and the park. The route goes from IMAX in the town of Tusayan, with stops at the Best Western Grand Canyon Squire Inn, the Grand Hotel, and Big E Steakhouse & Saloon, to the Grand Canyon Visitor

Center. Visitors riding the shuttle must have a park entrance pass, which can be purchased at several Tusayan businesses or the entrance station. The shuttle operates daily from Memorial Day to Labor Day from 8:00 a.m. to 9:30 p.m.

North Rim Shuttle

On the North Rim, a hikers' shuttle is available for a small fee. The shuttle departs from Grand Canyon Lodge and takes hikers to the often-full North Kaibab trailhead parking lot. The shuttle departs at 5:30 and 6:00 a.m. daily when the North Rim is in full swing, mid-May through mid-October. You must purchase tickets twenty-four hours in advance at the Grand Canyon Lodge front desk. This shuttle can be useful for hikers taking the Widforss Trail, Uncle Jim Trail, and the North Kaibab Trail to Supai Tunnel (Hikes 11, 12, and 13).

Items Every Hiker Should Carry

- 1-2 quarts of water per person, per hour of hiking
- First-aid kit including bandages and moleskin
- Sunscreen and lip balm
- Signal mirror
- Food
- Map
- Sweater or parka
- Rain gear or windproof parka
- Hat with brim
- Lightweight and durable hiking boots
- Toilet paper and resealable plastic bag for packing out used toilet paper, a National Park Service requirement

Ranking the Hikes

Plateau-Top Hikes
(Easiest to more challenging)
Rim Trail (South Rim)
Shoshone Point (South Rim)
Bright Angel Point (North Rim)
Cape Royal (North Rim)
Cliff Springs (North Rim)
Cape Final (North Rim)
Transept Trail (North Rim)
Bill Hall Trail to Monument Point (North Rim)
Ken Patrick Trail (North Rim)
Widforss Trail (North Rim)
Uncle Jim Trail (North Rim)

Hikes below the Rim
(Easiest to more challenging)
Bright Angel Trail to Mile-and-a-Half Resthouse (South Rim)
North Kaibab Trail to Supai Tunnel (North Rim)
South Kaibab Trail to Cedar Ridge (South Rim)
Hermits Rest to Dripping Springs (South Rim)
Hermits Rest to Santa Maria Spring (South Rim)
North Bass Trail to Muav Cabin (North Rim)

The South Rim

When most people envision the Grand Canyon, images of its South Rim come to mind. After all, the South Rim is the most photographed part of the Canyon, and calendars, postcards, and magazine articles have planted its panoramas in our minds. The vast majority of park visitors come to the South Rim for ample reasons. The South Rim offers an abundance of visitor services; it is easily accessible; and its vistas are among the finest in the park.

Panoramas of the Grand Canyon unfold to their greatest dimensions from the South Rim. Most often, air quality in the desert Southwest, including the Grand Canyon, is among the best in the nation. Night sky viewing is excellent. A visual range of 243 miles has been observed at the Grand Canyon, and it is not unusual to clearly see plateaus and the dome of Navajo Mountain in southern Utah from the South Rim, more than 100 miles distant. Hikers come to the South Rim in large numbers for many of these same reasons, plus the fact that most trailheads are easily accessible via paved roads. And there are more trails below the South Rim than elsewhere in the national park.

Unfortunately for hikers so much of the South Rim is claimed by roads and other developments that there are few opportunities for day hikes there. Yet there are two notable exceptions: the excellent Rim Trail and the closed road to Shoshone Point. Most South Rim day hikers descend into the Canyon and, of course, hike back out. Most hikers do not seem to mind this up-and-down trek, though, since the magnetic attraction of the Inner Canyon lures tens of thousands of day hikers onto South Rim trails each year.

Camping and Lodging

The South Rim is home to two fee campgrounds and an RV park. The 320-site Mather Campground, featuring water, toilets, tables, fire pits, and grills, is located south of Market Plaza in Grand Canyon Village. The campground is available on a first-come, first-served basis only from December 1 through March 1. At other times, you would be wise to book sites in advance. Reservations can be made by calling (877) 444-6777 or online at www.recreation.gov. The eighty-four-site Trailer Village adjacent to Mather Campground has RV hookups.

Desert View Campground, with water, tables, toilets, fire pits, and grills, has fifty sites on the South Rim at Desert View, 26 miles east of Grand Canyon Village on Desert View Drive. Sites are available on a first-come, first-served basis only.

Lodging is available in the lodges at Grand Canyon Village; make reservations well in advance by phoning (888) 297-2757 or visiting www.grandcanyonlodges.com.

For the Grand Canyon Lodge on the North Rim, call (877) 386-4383 or visit www.grandcanyonforever.com.

Visitors may also find lodging in the communities of Tusayan, Cameron, Valle, Flagstaff, and Williams.

Access

The South Rim is open year-round and can be reached from I-40 in the south. From Williams, drive north on AZ 64 for 59 miles to reach Grand Canyon Village. From Flagstaff follow US 180 and AZ 64 for 78 miles to the village. From the east, find the junction of AZ 64 and US 89 at Cameron, on the Navajo Indian Reservation. Cameron is located 82 miles south of Page, 58.3 miles south of the US 89/89A junction, and 16 miles south of the US 89/160 junction. Grand Canyon Village can be reached from Cameron by following AZ 64 west for 57 miles.

1 Shoshone Point

An easy out-and-back day hike leads to a glorious South Rim viewpoint.

Distance: 2.0 miles out and back
Hiking time: About 40 minutes to 1 hour
Elevation gain: 110 feet
Trail surface: Dirt road
Water availability: No water available

Best season: Apr through Nov
Canine compatibility: Leashed dogs permitted
Maps: *USGS Phantom Ranch; Trails Illustrated Grand Canyon National Park; Earthwalk Grand Canyon National Park*

Finding the trailhead: Find this unsigned trailhead along the north side of Desert View Drive, 3.5 miles east of the AZ 64/South Entrance Road junction and 1.3 miles east of the prominently signed Yaki Point turnoff. If you are approaching from the east via Desert View, note your odometer reading at the Grandview Point turnoff. You pass a picnic area on the north side of the road 2.7 miles west of the Grandview Point turnoff and reach the Shoshone Point Road and small parking area 6.3 miles west of the turnoff to Grandview Point. GPS N36 2.11' / W112 4.14'

The Hike

If time and energy allow you to hike only a few short trails on the South Rim, the trip to Shoshone Point, combining a walk through cool pine forests with truly dramatic vistas of the eastern Grand Canyon, should be at the top of your list.

The picnic area at the road's end is a popular spot for weddings, family gatherings, and other festivities. The site is available for day use by fee and permit from May 1 to October 15. Contact park headquarters at (928) 638-7707 or http://www.nps.gov/grca/learn/management/sup.htm for the information sheet on Shoshone Point. Before and after those dates, you'll likely have Shoshone Point to yourself. Hikers may check with park headquarters at the phone number above to check if private groups are using Shoshone Point on your planned hiking date. You can still hike if the area is reserved, just be aware that the picnic area at the end of the trail may be crowded.

The majority of South Rim viewpoints offer easy and short (yet often crowded and noisy) hikes from their paved parking lots. Seldom does a visitor enjoy quiet solitude when gazing across the vast depths of the Grand Canyon. Shoshone Point is a notable exception. Anyone willing to walk a 1.0-mile, nearly level dirt road will enjoy the opportunity to contemplate this great canyon in relative solitude. Perched high on the South Rim on a point of land dividing Grapevine and Cremation Canyons, Shoshone Point offers one of the finest vistas available from the South Rim.

Begin your walk at the locked gate on Shoshone Point Road. The road rises imperceptibly up a shallow draw beneath the shade of tall ponderosa pines. Gambel oaks and occasional piñons and junipers mix into the ranks of the pine forest. Typical of both rims of the Canyon, the forest signals your approach to the rim. The pines quickly diminish and are supplanted by a woodland of piñon and juniper. Shortly after entering this woodland, the road edges close to the east rim of the point. Soon you reach the loop at the road's end, where you find picnic tables, a large fire pit, fire grills, portable toilets, and garbage cans, facilities well used by visitors who have acquired permits to drive the dirt road in season.

A well-worn path ascends north beyond here and then descends another 150 yards among gnarled piñons and over slabs of Kaibab Formation rocks out to the point, where an unobstructed vista of the Grand Canyon unfolds, far from the crowds, noisy buses, and exhaust fumes of other South Rim viewpoints. Up canyon to the east you can see the foaming torrent of Hance Rapids, but elsewhere the river is blocked from your view by the Tapeats sandstone rim of the Inner Gorge. On the skyline beyond the rapids is Desert View Watchtower, and your eyes follow the east rim of the Canyon past the towering walls of the Palisades of the Desert to the distant Marble Platform and the Echo Cliffs.

Part of that view is obscured by the pyramidal crag of Vishnu Temple, one of the Canyon's most striking peaks. From Powell Plateau in the northwest, past Point Sublime to Cape Royal and Wotans Throne in the northeast, the forest-fringed North Rim and an incredible array of colorful buttes, mesas, and spires spread out before you.

Virtually at your feet the broad, dry wash of the east fork of Cremation Creek winds northwest and disappears into its Tapeats sandstone narrows above Granite Gorge. The switchbacks of the South Kaibab Trail through the Redwall limestone are clearly visible west of Cremation's broad desert basin. Clear Creek Canyon, with its own tortuous Vishnu Gorge, winds northeast beyond the invisible river, gathering waters from many-fingered canyons that reach up to the forested rim of Walhalla Plateau.

Lying far below is the wash of Boulder Creek, north of the point. To the east are the depths of Grapevine Creek, one of the South Rim's most extensive canyons. Other prominent features below the South Rim and east of the point include Horseshoe Mesa, Sinking Ship, Coronado Butte, and

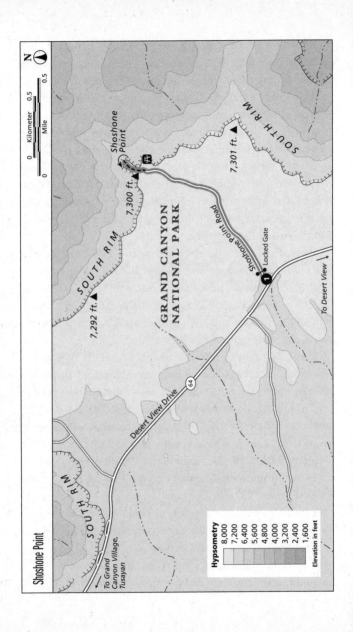

Shoshone Point

GRAND CANYON NATIONAL PARK

Shoshone Point

7,300 ft.

SOUTH RIM

7,292 ft.

SOUTH RIM

SOUTH RIM

7,301 ft.

Shoshone Point Road

Locked Gate

To Desert View

Desert View Drive

64

To Grand
Canyon Village,
Tusayan

Hypsometry

Elevation in feet
8,000
7,200
6,400
5,600
4,800
4,000
3,200
2,400
1,600

0   Kilometer   0.5

0   Mile   0.5

N

the distant red buttes of Escalante and Cardenas looming above the Tanner Trail.

While you are on the point, you may notice a grove of Douglas fir clinging to the foot of the Kaibab Formation cliff below the picnic area. More of these Canadian Zone trees can be seen to the west, occupying the Toroweap Formation slopes westward toward Yaki Point, between drought-tolerant bands of piñon and juniper. After enjoying the tremendous vistas, retrace your steps to the trailhead.

Miles and Directions

- **0.0** Start at the trailhead on Shoshone Point Road.
- **1.0** Shoshone Point; turnaround point.
- **2.0** Arrive back at the trailhead on Shoshone Point Road.

2 South Kaibab Trail to Cedar Ridge

A view-packed half-day out-and-back hike below the South Rim follows one of the most popular—and more challenging—trails in the Grand Canyon.

Distance: 2.8 miles out and back

Hiking time: About 3 hours

Elevation gain: 1,150 feet

Trail surface: Maintained; excellent condition

Water availability: No water available on trail; available at trailhead May through Sept

Best season: Mar though June; Sept through Nov

Other trail users: Mules

Canine compatibility: Dogs not permitted

Maps: *USGS Phantom Ranch; Trails Illustrated Grand Canyon National Park; Earthwalk Grand Canyon National Park*

Finding the trailhead: The road to Yaki Point and the South Kaibab trailhead is closed to private vehicles. Hikers must ride the free Kaibab Trail Route shuttle bus, which departs every 15 minutes from Canyon View Information Plaza. The well-signed information plaza is located 23 miles west of Desert View and about a mile east of Grand Canyon Village. There is also an early-morning hikers express shuttle from Bright Angel and Maswik Lodges to Yaki Point and the South Kaibab trailhead. Check the park newspaper (given to you when you enter the park) for current times for this shuttle. Or park at the Pipe Creek Vista viewpoint and hike 0.8 mile east along the Rim Trail to the South Kaibab trailhead. South Kaibab trailhead GPS N36 3.18' / W112 5.04'; Pipe Creek Vista GPS N36 2.84' / W 112 5.47'

The Hike

The South Kaibab Trail is a must-do for Grand Canyon visitors wishing to see the Canyon from the inside out. Hikers flock to this excellent trail in a steady stream for much of the year, and the majority of trail users are day hikers making the rewarding trip to Cedar Ridge. A continuum of tremendous vistas unfold with every step of the way. The trail, one of the most popular day hikes in the park, is moderately steep and shadeless. Unlike the Bright Angel Trail, no drinking water is available below the rim. Mule trains returning from the Bright Angel Trail and Phantom Ranch use the trail daily. When you encounter mules, step quietly off the trail and allow them to pass, and follow the instructions of the wrangler.

From the trailhead parking lot, follow the trail north past the mule corrals for several yards to the piñon- and juniper-clad South Rim. Here, next to a pay telephone and interpretive signboard, the South Kaibab Trail begins its plunge into the Grand Canyon. A series of wide switchbacks leads down through the gray limestone cliff band of the Kaibab Formation at a moderate grade. In winter, when the trail is covered with snow or ice, the wide trail is still reasonably safe and easy to follow, though the use of some type of snow-traction device such as YakTrax is strongly recommended.

At the foot of the Kaibab cliff, hikers traverse north upon the steep red slopes of the Toroweap Formation. Here piñons and junipers reappear, along with an occasional Douglas fir in sheltered recesses. Pipe Creek Canyon lies far below the trail, and shady alcoves at its head also support Douglas fir, growing in an extensive grove. On the northernmost switchback Ooh Aah Point provides a splendid view and optional turnaround point for a shorter hike.

Where the trail rounds the shoulder of Cedar Ridge, you reach the sparkling Coconino sandstone. Follow the rocky trail steadily downhill, switching back from one side of the

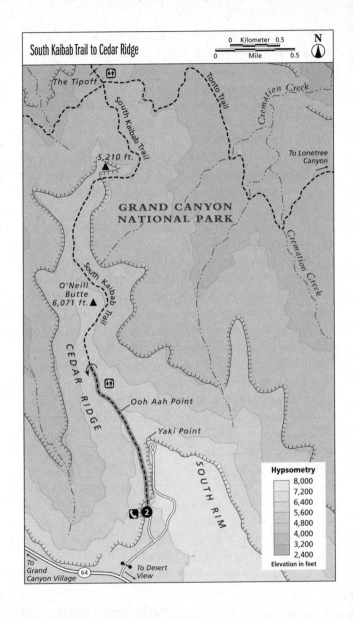

South Kaibab Trail to Cedar Ridge

0   Kilometer   0.5
0   Mile   0.5

N

The Tipoff

South Kaibab Trail

Tonto Trail

Cremation Creek

5,210 ft.

GRAND CANYON
NATIONAL PARK

To Lonetree
Canyon

South Kaibab Trail

Cremation Creek

O'Neill
Butte
6,071 ft.

South Kaibab Trail

CEDAR RIDGE

Ooh Aah Point

Yaki Point

SOUTH RIM

2

To
Grand
Canyon Village

64

To Desert
View

Hypsometry

8,000
7,200
6,400
5,600
4,800
4,000
3,200
2,400

Elevation in feet

ridge to the other. O'Neill Butte, capped by a block of red Esplanade sandstone, looms ahead as you stroll down the red slopes of the Hermit Formation to the broad, piñon- and juniper-studded platform of Cedar Ridge at 6,050 feet. Soon you will pass the composting toilets and reach a dramatic vista point, the goal of most day hikers on the trail.

A boot-worn trail leads 300 yards northwest to the point of the ridge, which affords even broader panoramas. Pipe Creek Canyon lies far below to the west, and one can visually trace the course of the Tonto Trail as it traverses that creek's basin en route to Indian Garden. The Devil's Corkscrew on the Bright Angel Trail is visible as it descends from the hanging valley of Garden Creek into the dark Vishnu schist hallway of lower Pipe Creek.

The broad, blackbrush-studded basin of Cremation Creek spreads out below and to the east of your vantage point. Far beyond rises the barrier wall of the Palisades of the Desert, and Desert View Watchtower can be seen capping the eastern end of the South Rim. The forest-fringed North Rim provides a backdrop for your Canyon vista. To the northeast, the erosion-isolated mesa of Wotans Throne and the slender spire of Vishnu Temple rise in bold relief.

From Cedar Ridge, backtrack to the trailhead.

Miles and Directions

0.0   Start at the South Kaibab trailhead.

0.9   Reach Ooh Aah Point.

1.4   Arrive at Cedar Ridge; turnaround point.

2.8   Arrive back at the South Kaibab trailhead.

3 Bright Angel Trail to Mile-and-a-Half Resthouse

A very scenic half-day out–and–back hike travels below the South Rim along the Grand Canyon's most popular trail.

Distance: 3.0 miles out and back

Hiking time: About 2 to 3 hours

Elevation gain: 1,120 feet

Trail surface: Maintained; excellent condition

Water availability: Available May through Sept at Mile-and-a-Half Resthouse

Best season: Mar through June; Sept through Nov

Other trail users: Mules

Canine compatibility: Dogs not permitted

Maps: *USGS Grand Canyon; Trails Illustrated Grand Canyon National Park; Earthwalk Bright Angel Trail or Grand Canyon National Park*

Finding the trailhead: The Bright Angel Trail begins just west of Kolb Studio on the South Rim, immediately northeast of the Hermits Rest Transfer shuttle bus stop. No parking is available at the trailhead. Hikers must park at either the public parking lot adjacent to Maswik Lodge, 0.2 mile south of Bright Angel Lodge, or in one of the large parking areas south of the railroad tracks between Bright Angel Lodge and the train depot.

To reach the Bright Angel Lodge area and the Hermits Rest Transfer shuttle bus stop, follow the South Entrance Road for 2.75 miles from the junction with Desert View Drive to a Y junction in Grand Canyon Village. Bear right at that junction onto one-way Village Loop Road, prominently signed for El Tovar and Bright Angel Lodge. Follow the road past the train depot and hotel complex for another 0.6 mile to the Hermits Rest Transfer shuttle bus stop. Turn left (south) to reach the public parking areas within another 0.2 mile. GPS N36 3.44' / W112 8.62'

The Hike

The Bright Angel Trail is the most popular trail in the park and one of the most beautiful. Splendid vistas; an excellent, well-groomed trail; and a shady resthouse located just far enough below the rim for hikers to gain the feel and appreciate the dimensions of the Inner Canyon combine to make this hike an excellent choice for first-time Grand Canyon hikers.

Although water is seasonally available at the resthouse, breaks in the water pipeline occasionally occur. Hikers are strongly advised to carry their own water. Mule trains use this trail each day to descend into the Canyon en route to Plateau Point and Phantom Ranch. As a result of this heavy downhill traffic, the trail is rougher than the South Kaibab Trail, and the tread has developed a corrugated surface.

The trail begins immediately northeast of the Hermits Rest Transfer shuttle bus stop, a short distance west of the Bright Angel Lodge complex. Follow the trail as it descends below the rim, avoiding the right-branching spur of the Rim Trail within the first several yards. Beyond the first switchback, you pass through a tunnel carved into the Kaibab Formation. Look for a pictograph panel, believed to be of Havasupai origin, several yards above the trail beyond the tunnel. Although the Bright Angel Trail follows a canyon route, excellent views are nevertheless enjoyed from the beginning. Far below lies Indian Garden, an oasis surrounded by the blackbrush flats of the Tonto Platform. The Plateau Point Trail appears as a wide white scar across the Tonto Platform beyond Indian Garden.

The Bright Angel Fault, a prominent feature in this part of the Grand Canyon, is one of many faults in the Canyon that have altered the generally flat-lying layers of sedimentary rock. It stretches northeast from the Coconino Plateau to the Kaibab Plateau. Garden Creek below you and the distant trough of Bright Angel Canyon were eroded along this zone of shattered rock. The cliffs that bound the headwaters amphitheater of Garden Creek are noticeably offset by movement along the fault. The cliffs to the west were uplifted nearly 200 feet relative to the cliffs east of the canyon. The resulting break in the cliff bands has been used by humans for centuries to reach the Inner Canyon.

After two long switchbacks through the Toroweap Formation, you pass through a second short tunnel and then reach the Coconino sandstone. Here a series of short, moderately steep switchbacks leads down through the fault-controlled break in the Coconino cliff. Garden Creek's drainage has carved a steep gully in this break, through which the trail descends among a jumble of shattered blocks. A scattering of Douglas fir appears in the cool, shady microclimate that prevails at the base of the gully.

Beyond the switchbacks, a steadily descending traverse of steep, red Hermit Formation slopes leads down to Mile-and-a-Half Resthouse, tucked away in a shady recess. Seasonal drinking water, toilets, and an emergency telephone are available here. From the resthouse you can visually trace the cavernous course of Bright Angel Creek, carved along the arrow-straight line of the Bright Angel Fault, as it reaches far back toward the North Rim. An array of varicolored buttes and towers, including Sumner Butte, Cheops Pyramid, and Brahma Temple, punctuate the middle distance.

Return to the rim the way you came.

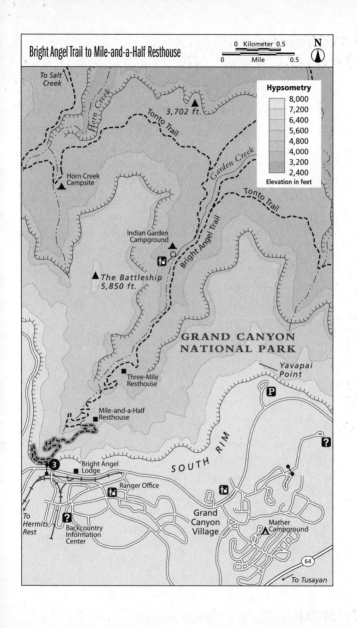

Bright Angel Trail to Mile-and-a-Half Resthouse

0   Kilometer   0.5

0   Mile   0.5

N

Hypsometry

8,000
7,200
6,400
5,600
4,800
4,000
3,200
2,400
Elevation in feet

To Salt Creek

Horn Creek

Tonto Trail

3,702 ft.

Garden Creek

Horn Creek Campsite

Tonto Trail

Bright Angel Trail

Indian Garden Campground

The Battleship 5,850 ft.

GRAND CANYON NATIONAL PARK

Yavapai Point

Three-Mile Resthouse

Mile-and-a-Half Resthouse

SOUTH RIM

Bright Angel Lodge

Ranger Office

To Hermits Rest

Backcountry Information Center

Grand Canyon Village

Mather Campground

64

To Tusayan

Miles and Directions

0.0 Start at the Bright Angel trailhead.

1.5 Arrive at Mile-and-a-Half Resthouse; turnaround point.

3.0 Arrive back at the Bright Angel trailhead.

4 Rim Trail

The best easy hike on the South Rim offers a continuum of dramatic canyon views.

Distance: Variable; up to 11.8 miles point to point
Hiking time: Variable
Elevation gain: 425 feet
Trail surface: Paved from Pipe Creek Vista to Maricopa Point; unmaintained, in fair condition, from Maricopa Point to Hermits Rest
Water availability: Available at Yavapai Point, lodges in Grand Canyon Village, and Hermits Rest.

Bring your own, especially on hikes west of the village.
Best season: Apr through Oct
Other trail users: Bicycles
Canine compatibility: Leashed dogs permitted
Maps: USGS Phantom Ranch and Grand Canyon; Trails Illustrated Grand Canyon National Park; Earthwalk Grand Canyon National Park (entire trail shown only on Earthwalk map)

Finding the trailhead: This trail can be reached from fourteen different access points. From east to west they are Pipe Creek Vista, Mather Point, Yavapai Point, Canyon View Information Station, the El Tovar/Bright Angel Lodge complex, Bright Angel Trailhead/Hermits Rest Transfer shuttle bus stop, Trailview Overlook, Maricopa Point, Powell Memorial, Hopi Point, Mohave Point, The Abyss overlook, Pima Point, and Hermits Rest. Hikers on the Rim Trail usually follow the trail for a short distance from one of these access points, then either backtrack to their cars or take advantage of the park's free shuttle bus system.

Perhaps the best way to hike segments of the Rim Trail is to park in the public parking areas near Bright Angel Lodge (south of Hermits Rest Transfer shuttle bus stop) and either begin hiking from there and return via a shuttle bus or ride a bus to another access point and hike back to your car.

To reach the Bright Angel Lodge area and the Hermits Rest Transfer shuttle bus stop, follow South Entrance Road for 2.75 miles from the junction with Desert View Drive to a Y junction in Grand Canyon Village. Bear right at that junction onto one-way Village Loop Road, prominently signed for El Tovar and Bright Angel Lodge. Follow the road past the train depot and hotel complex for another 0.6 mile to the Hermits Rest Transfer shuttle bus stop. Turn left (south) to reach the public parking areas within another 0.2 mile.

When you enter the national park, be sure to obtain a copy of the *Guide,* the park's information newspaper, which shows a map of the trail and gives information regarding shuttle buses and bus stop locations. Pipe Creek Vista trailhead GPS N36 2.84' / W 112° 5.47'; Hermits Rest trailhead GPS N36 3.64' / W112 12.74'

The Hike

The scenic Rim Trail is arguably Grand Canyon National Park's finest easy day hike. Nowhere else in the park do Grand Canyon vistas unfold in such breathtaking dimensions. Although the trail often closely follows park roads, segments of the trail (notably, between Yavapai Point and the lodge complex, and between The Abyss and Pima Point) deviate from the course of the road, allowing hikers to enjoy interesting perspectives of the Canyon in comparative solitude.

Note: The Miles and Directions for this hike cover the trail from Pipe Creek to Hermits Rest.

Pipe Creek Vista to Yavapai Point, 1.9 miles

This segment begins at Pipe Creek Vista, a westbound shuttle stop on the Kaibab Trail Route shuttle. The trail hugs the rim for much of the way to Mather Point, so exercise appropriate caution. Vistas are outstanding, reaching more than 4,000 feet into the dramatic gorge of Pipe Creek.

After 1.3 miles, the trail edges close to the large parking area at Mather Point. Hikers wishing to visit the Canyon View Information Plaza can take a spur trail leading about 300 yards south across Desert View Drive.

Between Mather and Yavapai Points, you are likely to share the trail with many others. More sweeping vistas stretch across Pipe Creek Canyon toward the North Rim.

Yavapai Point to the lodge complex, 1.4 miles

From the Yavapai Observation Station, the Rim Trail curves left and follows the edge of the wooded South Rim high above Garden Creek Canyon. After 0.8 mile, a signed trail branches left (south), leading 0.4 mile to the park head-quarters complex. The final 0.6 mile of this segment affords fine views into the depths of Garden Creek, past an array of colorful Inner Canyon buttes to the bold cliffs and terraces that stair-step up to the distant North Rim. After 1.4 miles you reach the east end of the lodge complex at Verkamp's Visitor Center.

Verkamp's to the Bright Angel trailhead, 0.4 mile

This flat segment is the busiest part of the trail, passing the historic buildings of Verkamp's Visitor Center, Hopi House (built around the turn of the twentieth century in the Pueblo style), El Tovar Hotel, Bright Angel Lodge, and Kolb Studio. Vistas, as usual along the Rim Trail, are panoramic, affording aerial-like views into the Grand Canyon, including the cottonwood-shaded oasis of Indian Garden far below.

Bright Angel trailhead to Maricopa Point, 1.4 miles

This segment of the Rim Trail gradually ascends the West Rim to Maricopa Point. As the trail hugs the rim, it affords fine views of hikers far below on the switchbacks of the Bright Angel Trail. You will be joined by many other hikers after passing Trailview Overlook after 0.5 mile. Shortly beyond the Maricopa Point parking area, after 1.1 miles, the pavement ends at Maricopa Point proper.

Maricopa Point to Hermits Rest, 6.7 miles

Best done in two or three shorter segments for a leisurely hike, the Rim Trail section between Maricopa Point and Hermits Rest is perhaps the most dramatic and interesting part of its route. The unpaved trail is often narrow and much less frequently used than previous segments. Exercise care, as the trail often clings to steep slopes and the very edge of plunging cliffs.

From Maricopa Point the trail leads past the old buildings of the Lost Orphan Mine, a rich uranium mine dating back to the 1950s uranium boom. That area is closed to the public. About 200 yards beyond the mine, you reach another parking area and the very short spur trail to Powell Point. The spur trail offers another fine Canyon panorama and a memorial placed in honor of John Wesley Powell and his epic 1869 expedition down the Colorado River.

The Rim Trail continues on to Hopi Point after another 0.8 mile. Beyond the point, a new perspective of the Canyon unfolds, and vistas stretch far downcanyon to distant Powell Plateau and the dome of Mount Trumbull. Frequent views of the Colorado River far below, including the foaming cauldrons of Granite and Hermit Rapids, help illustrate the Canyon's immense depth. The sinuous Tonto Trail is occasionally visible, traversing the desert terrace of the Tonto Platform about 3,500 feet below.

After 1.6 miles the path curves around Mohave Point, then follows the rim far back toward the head of The Abyss. This aptly named void is notable not only for its broad, colorful, 3,000-foot-deep amphitheater but also for its unusual

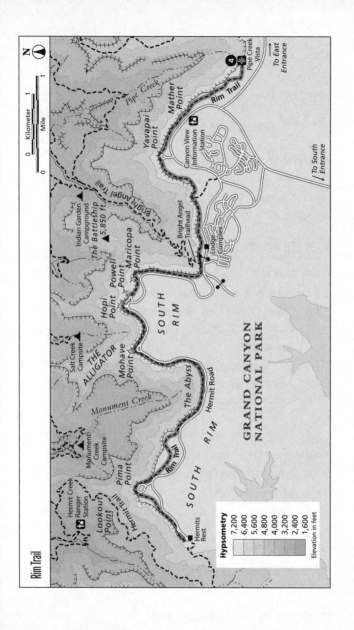

Rim Trail

GRAND CANYON NATIONAL PARK

Hypsometry

| 7,200 |
| 6,400 |
| 5,600 |
| 4,800 |
| 4,000 |
| 3,200 |
| 2,400 |
| 1,600 |

Elevation in feet

N

0   Kilometer   1
0   Mile   1

Pipe Creek
Mather Point
Yavapai Point
Rim Trail
Pipe Creek Vista
To East Entrance

Bright Angel Trail
Indian Garden Campground
The Battleship 5,850 ft.
Maricopa Point
Powell Point
Hopi Point
Canyon View Information Station
To South Entrance

Bright Angel Trailhead
Lodge Complex

SOUTH RIM

THE ALLIGATOR
Salt Creek Campsite
Mohave Point

Monument Creek
Hermit Creek Ranger Station
Monument Creek Campsite
Lookout Point
Hermit Trail
Pima Point

The Abyss
Hermit Road
Rim Trail

SOUTH RIM

Hermits Rest

groves of Douglas fir, a high-elevation conifer common on the Kaibab Plateau but found here only in the coolest micro-climates below the South Rim cliffs. Like the Tonto Trail far below, the Rim Trail must detour around the gaping void of The Abyss. The 4.0 miles from Mohave Point to Pima Point (at 10.7 miles) are long yet spectacular.

The final 1.1-mile leg of the Rim Trail from Pima Point to Hermits Rest affords tremendous views into Hermit Creek Canyon and to Hermit and Boucher Rapids. Once you reach the Hermits Rest parking area, board the next bus and return to the Hermits Rest Transfer shuttle bus stop.

Miles and Directions

- **0.0** Start at the Pipe Creek Vista trailhead.
- **1.3** Arrive at the parking area at Mather Point.
- **1.9** Come to Yavapai Point observation station.
- **2.7** Reach junction with left-branching trail to park headquarters. Stay straight.
- **3.3** Enter lodge complex.
- **3.7** Pass Bright Angel trailhead/Village Route Transfer/Hermits Rest Transfer; continue straight ahead alongside West Rim Drive.
- **5.1** Ascend the West Rim to Maricopa Point; end of paved trail.
- **5.6** Pass Powell Point and Powell Memorial.
- **5.9** Continue to Hopi Point.
- **6.7** Curve around Mohave Point.
- **7.8** The Abyss overlook includes a view of the 3,000-foot-deep amphitheater.
- **10.7** Pass Pima Point.
- **11.8** Arrive at the parking area at Hermits Rest; end of trail.

5 Hermits Rest to Santa Maria Spring

A more challenging, but rewarding day hike traverses below the western reaches of the South Rim.

Distance: 4.6 miles out and back
Hiking time: About 3 to 4 hours
Elevation gain: 1,640 feet
Trail surface: Unmaintained; generally good condition
Water availability: Available at Hermits Rest. Santa Maria Spring at 2.25 miles offers a trickling seep, but because water must be treated, bring your own.
Best season: Mar through June; Sept through Nov
Canine compatibility: Dogs not permitted
Maps: USGS Grand Canyon; Trails Illustrated Grand Canyon National Park; Earthwalk Grand Canyon National Park

Finding the trailhead: From Mar 1 through Nov 30, Hermit Road is closed to private vehicles. During this time, a free shuttle bus offers access to Hermits Rest every 15 and 30 minutes from about 5:15 a.m. to sunset each day. You can board the shuttle bus at the Hermits Rest Transfer shuttle bus stop.

To reach the Bright Angel Lodge area and the Hermits Rest Transfer shuttle bus stop, follow the South Entrance Road for 2.75 miles from the junction with Desert View Drive to a Y junction in Grand Canyon Village. Bear right at that junction onto one-way Village Loop Road, prominently signed for El Tovar and Bright Angel Lodge. Follow the road past the train depot and hotel complex for another 0.6 mile to the Hermits Rest Transfer shuttle bus stop. Turn left (south) to reach the public parking areas within another 0.2 mile.

Drinking water, toilets, garbage receptacles, a pay telephone, pop machine, snack bar, and curio shop are available at Hermits Rest. GPS N36 3.64' / W112 12.74'

The Hike

This fine trip follows a trail constructed by the Santa Fe Railroad in 1912 and leads to the shady resthouse at Santa Maria Spring, perched high above the abyss of Hermit Creek Canyon. Although the trail was abandoned in 1931 and the tread is generally rougher than the groomed Corridor trails, it remains easy to follow as far as the spring.

The abrupt cliffs of the South Rim have been softened by time below Hermits Rest, and the Hermit Trail takes advantage of this break as it descends a moderate yet rocky grade through piñon-juniper woodlands below the road's end. After dropping into a shallow draw, the trail switchbacks briefly through the Kaibab Formation, then begins a southbound traverse over red and gray Toroweap Formation slopes. Piñon and juniper are joined on the trailside slopes by a shrub cover of cliffrose, littleleaf mountain mahogany, and sagebrush. Exciting views begin to unfold here, reaching across the gaping red abyss of Hermit Creek Canyon to the soaring cliffs that bound the wooded hanging valley of Hermit Basin.

The traverse ends upon reaching the sparkling sandstone of the broken Coconino cliff. Switchbacks ensue, leading steadily downhill over ledges and slabs. The steeper pitches here are paved with cobbles, allowing the tread to withstand the ravages of erosion. Keep an eye out for fossil reptile tracks on trailside slabs; they are more obvious here than along any other Grand Canyon trail. Mats of scrub live oak join various other shrubs here. Along with abundant piñon and juniper, woodland shrubs and small trees form a drab green veneer that engulfs Hermit Basin and obscures much of the

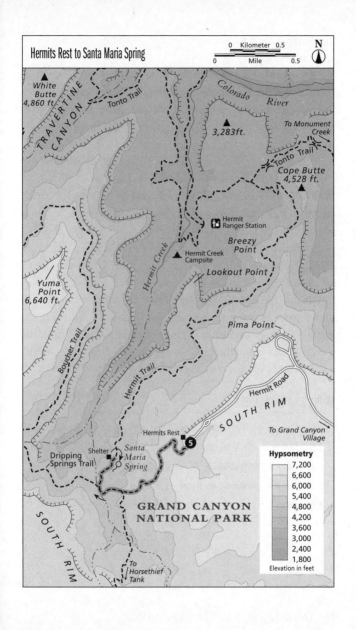

Hermits Rest to Santa Maria Spring

0   Kilometer   0.5

0   Mile   0.5

N

White
Butte
4,860 ft.

TRAVERTINE CANYON

Tonto Trail

Colorado   River

3,283 ft.

To Monument
Creek

Tonto Trail

Cope Butte
4,528 ft.

Hermit
Ranger Station

Hermit Creek

Breezy
Point

Hermit Creek
Campsite

Lookout Point

Yuma
Point
6,640 ft.

Boucher Trail

Pima Point

Hermit Trail

Hermit Road

SOUTH RIM

Hermits Rest

5

To Grand Canyon
Village

Dripping
Springs Trail

Shelter

Santa
Maria
Spring

SOUTH RIM

GRAND CANYON
NATIONAL PARK

To
Horsethief
Tank

Hypsometry

| 7,200 |
| 6,600 |
| 6,000 |
| 5,400 |
| 4,800 |
| 4,200 |
| 3,600 |
| 3,000 |
| 2,400 |
| 1,800 |

Elevation in feet

Canyon's upper rock layers, lending a softer appearance to the landscape.

After emerging onto the red slopes of the Hermit Formation that flank Hermit Basin, the trail begins a straightforward, steep, and rocky descent past the signed junction with the seldom-used Waldron Trail at 5,400 feet. Finally the grade moderates in the wash on the basin floor. At the junction here (at 5,200 feet), turn right. The trail ahead continues west to the Boucher Trail and Dripping Springs.

From the junction, short switchbacks lead down to the crossing of the dry wash, where the trail is funneled between two slickrock pour-offs. The trail ahead descends 250 feet in 0.5 mile, with the aid of a few switchbacks, to the Santa Maria Spring Resthouse. This long, roofed shelter, draped by an arbor of canyon wild grape, offers a welcome refuge from the sun. The spring, however, is a mere trickle. It offers enough water for a drink, but filling a bottle requires a long-term commitment. Do not drink water from the spring without purification. From the pleasant shade of the resthouse, return the way you came.

Miles and Directions

0.0 Start at the Hermits Rest trailhead parking area.

1.5 Junction with Waldron Trail; stay right.

1.8 Junction with Dripping Springs Trail; bear right.

2.3 Arrive at Santa Maria Spring; turnaround point.

4.6 Arrive back at the Hermits Rest trailhead parking area.

6 Hermits Rest to Dripping Springs

A more challenging out-and-back day hike below the South Rim leads to an aptly named spring.

Distance: 6.6 miles out and back

Hiking time: About 4 to 5 hours

Elevation gain: 1,490 feet

Trail surface: Unmaintained; generally good condition

Water availability: Available at Hermits Rest and Dripping Springs (must be treated before drinking); bring your own

Best season: Mar through June; Sept through Nov

Canine compatibility: Dogs not permitted

Maps: *USGS Grand Canyon; Trails Illustrated Grand Canyon National Park; Earthwalk Grand Canyon National Park*

Finding the trailhead: From Mar 1 through Nov 30, Hermit Road is closed to private vehicles. During this time a free shuttle bus offers access to Hermits Rest every 15 and 30 minutes from about 5:15 a.m. to sunset every day. You can board the shuttle bus at Hermits Rest Transfer shuttle bus stop. To reach the shuttle bus stop, follow South Entrance Road for 2.75 miles from the junction with Desert View Drive to a Y junction in Grand Canyon Village. Bear right at that junction onto one-way Village Loop Road, prominently signed for El Tovar and Bright Angel Lodge. Follow the road past the train depot and hotel complex for another 0.6 mile to the Hermits Rest Transfer shuttle bus stop. Turn left (south) to reach the public parking areas within another 0.2 mile.

There are two alternative ways to reach the spring: via the Waldron Trail and via Louis Boucher's original Dripping Springs Trail. Those trails can be reached by following a confusing network of park roads west from the Village Picnic Area, but they are seldom used. Finding the trailheads requires map-reading skills as well as driving skills on exceedingly rough and rocky four-wheel-drive roads. Contact the Backcountry Information Center for directions if you are determined to use one of those trails. GPS N36 3.64' / W112 12.74'

The Hike

The hike to Dripping Springs via the Hermit Trail is one of the best day trips on the South Rim. The trail offers a good introduction to the nature of Grand Canyon trails, as well as dramatic vistas, and ends at an unusual spring where water rains from the roof of an alcove at the base of the Coconino sandstone. Hikers should carry ample water for the round-trip, since water from Dripping Springs must be treated before drinking.

From the Hermits Rest trailhead parking area, follow the Hermit Trail, descending 1,450 feet in 1.8 miles and about one hour to Hermit Basin. At 1.5 miles you come to the junction with Waldron Trail; stay right to continue to Dripping Springs Trail. From the signed junction, bear left toward Dripping Springs and the Boucher Trail. The following 1.0 mile of trail is an exciting stretch that undulates along the steep slopes of the red Hermit Formation. The trail is, by necessity, funneled between the sheer, 1,200-foot Kaibab–Toroweap Formation–Coconino cliffs above and the 800-foot Supai cliffs below.

With minor undulations, the trail curves into two prominent, shadowed amphitheaters that host a rich woodland of tall, spreading shrubs and small trees, such as pale hoptree, Utah serviceberry, alder-leaf mountain mahogany, Fremont barberry, mock orange, squaw currant, and single-leaf ash. The Supai cliffs at the trail's edge plummet into the narrows of upper Hermit Creek Canyon far below, lying in the near-perpetual shade of towering Redwall cliffs. The North Rim, cool and forested, rises in the distance behind innumerable buttes, towers, and terraces.

At length you enter the wooded lower reaches of the Dripping Springs draw, where you meet the northbound Boucher Trail. Bear left at the junction and begin a moderate ascent west up the draw through open woodland of piñon, juniper, cliffrose, scrub live oak, fragrant ash, Apache plume, and other shrubs. The draw ahead appears to dead-end in an amphitheater embraced by bulging, cross-bedded walls of Coconino sandstone, stained with veils of brown desert varnish. Soon you reach the head of the amphitheater and then curve into its sheltered alcove. Here, beneath the overhanging sandstone walls, you find Dripping Springs.

True to its name, the spring drips from the roof of the alcove, decorated with clumps of maidenhair fern, into a small, rock-framed pool fringed by the nodding blooms of scarlet monkeyflower. Other seeps, also fringed with ferns, emerge from the walls of the alcove, a few feet above the Coconino sandstone/Hermit Formation contact zone. Ample shade is cast by the alcove's overhanging walls and by the thickets of shrubs and netleaf hackberry trees that surround it. Coconino cliffs rise 300 to 400 feet above this peaceful locale, where you will likely enjoy the aerial acrobatics of white-throated swifts and violet-green swallows, and perhaps hear the melancholy song of a canyon wren.

Louis Boucher maintained a tent camp and corrals on the bench below the spring from the 1890s to about 1912. Nature has since reclaimed the site, and now the bench hosts the spreading foliage of netleaf hackberry and redbud trees. (No camping is allowed here or elsewhere along the trail.) Boucher's original trail continues east through the alcove

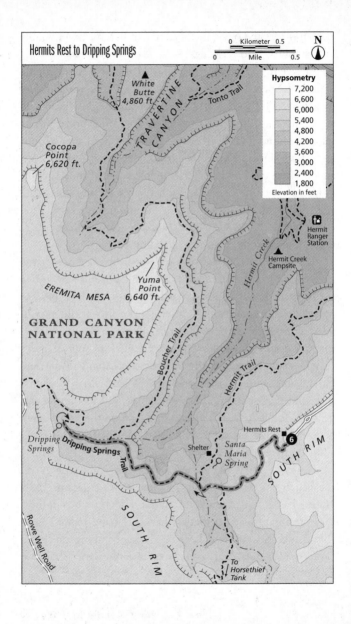

Hermits Rest to Dripping Springs

0 Kilometer 0.5
0 Mile 0.5

N

Hypsometry

7,200
6,600
6,000
5,400
4,800
4,200
3,600
3,000
2,400
1,800
Elevation in feet

▲ White Butte
4,860 ft.

TRAVERTINE CANYON

Tonto Trail

Cocopa Point
6,620 ft.

Hermit Creek

Hermit Ranger Station

▲ Hermit Creek Campsite

EREMITA MESA

Yuma Point
6,640 ft.

GRAND CANYON NATIONAL PARK

Boucher Trail

Hermit Trail

Dripping Springs

Dripping Springs Trail

Shelter

Santa Maria Spring

Hermits Rest

6

SOUTH RIM

Rowe Well Road

SOUTH RIM

To Horsethief Tank

beyond Dripping Springs, then ascends 800 feet in 1.3 miles to the remote trailhead atop the South Rim.

From Dripping Springs, return the way you came.

Miles and Directions

0.0 Start at the Hermits Rest trailhead parking area.

1.5 Junction with Waldron Trail; stay right.

1.8 Junction of Hermit and Dripping Springs Trails; bear left.

2.8 Junction with northbound Boucher Trail; stay left.

3.3 Arrive at Dripping Springs; turnaround point.

6.6 Arrive back at the Hermits Rest trailhead parking area.

The North Rim

The North Rim of the Grand Canyon forms an alluring backdrop to vistas from the South Rim. Its fringe of tall conifers holds the promise of a cool refuge from desert heat and solitude in a wilderness setting. The North Rim has an atmosphere of great remoteness and unspoiled grandeur. It is this remoteness that makes it such a special place.

Separated from the South Rim by only 10 to 18 miles as the crow flies, the North Rim can be reached in two ways: either by hiking 22 to 24 miles across the Grand Canyon, which often requires a raft to ferry across the river, or by driving 215 miles around it. The North Rim lies at the end of a long dead-end road that traverses the rich conifer forests and grassy parks of the Kaibab Plateau, many miles from the nearest enclaves of civilization. Though the North Rim receives only one tenth the number of visitors as the South Rim, fewer roads and visitor services here concentrate use so that places here can seem congested at times.

Canyon overlooks on national park roads at the North Rim are not as abundant as on the South Rim, where it seems every bend in the road presents an incredible vista. As if to compensate for fewer overlooks, North Rim viewpoints afford vistas of the Grand Canyon that are consistently awe-inspiring and overwhelming, even to the most jaded canyoneer. Fringed with forests of pine, fir, spruce, and aspen, North Rim overlooks survey a remarkable landscape of colorful cliffs, bold towers, deep labyrinths, and seemingly barren desert.

Most North Rim trails are as lonely as the nearby overlooks are congested. Only one maintained trail descends into the Grand Canyon from the North Rim, and this—the North Kaibab Trail—receives the bulk of use here for good reasons. The North Kaibab is an excellent, highly scenic trail that offers something for everyone, from the visitor out for a stroll to the backpacker plunging into the Grand Canyon's depths.

Numerous trails atop the Kaibab Plateau at the North Rim offer fine day hiking opportunities. These trails are an excellent choice for summer-season hikers wishing to avoid the overwhelming heat of the Inner Canyon yet still enjoy incomparable views. The North Rim boasts the highest concentration of plateau-top trails in the park. Hikers can spend several days traversing them all or spend only an hour or two on one of the many rewarding short trails. These trails are easy to follow and are among the best of the Grand Canyon's easy day hikes.

Camping

The eighty-two-site North Rim Campground, open from mid-May through mid-October, is the only campground on the North Rim of the Grand Canyon. Facilities in this fee campground include water, tables, toilets, fire pits, and grills. Some sites may be available at your time of arrival, but to ensure you get a site, make reservations by calling (877) 444-6777 or at www.recreation.gov.

Kaibab National Forest is open to at-large camping, and many excellent sites can be found along almost any forest road. Campers must be aware of fire restrictions (if applicable) and off-road travel restrictions and must camp at least 0.25 mile from paved roads and water sources.

Access

The North Rim is closed by snow each winter and is usually open from May 15 through late October only. To reach the North Rim from the east, follow US 89 south from Page for 25.8 miles, or take it 58.3 miles north from Cameron to the junction with US 89A. Follow US 89A north, then west, for 57.25 miles to Jacob Lake on the Kaibab Plateau at the junction with southbound AZ 67 (also known as the Kaibab Plateau–North Rim Parkway). Jacob Lake can also be reached from the north via US 89A, 29.8 miles south of the US 89A/AZ 389 junction in Fredonia and 34 miles south of US 89 in Kanab, Utah. The North Rim Entrance Station is 31 miles south of Jacob Lake via AZ 67. The road ends at Grand Canyon Lodge, 11.7 miles south of the entrance station.

7 Ken Patrick Trail

A half-day, moderate day hike travels along the east rim of the Kaibab Plateau.

Distance: 6.0 miles out and back

Hiking time: About 3 to 4 hours

Elevation gain: 369 feet

Trail surface: Unmaintained; good condition

Water availability: No water available

Best season: Mid-May through mid-Oct

Canine compatibility: Dogs not permitted

Maps: *USGS Point Imperial* (trail not shown on map); *Trails Illustrated Grand Canyon National Park*

Finding the trailhead: From the North Rim Entrance Station, proceed into the park for 9.5 miles to the junction with Cape Royal/Point Imperial Road. Turn left and follow the narrow, winding pavement for 5.4 miles to a Y junction, then bear left toward Point Imperial. You will reach the Point Imperial parking area after another 2.7 miles.

The Ken Patrick Trail crosses Cape Royal Road 1.0 mile from the Y junction. One-way hikers can shuttle a car or arrange for a pickup at a turnout 0.1 mile west of where the trail crosses the road. GPS N36 16.71' / W 111 58.73'

The Hike

The Ken Patrick Trail stretches 10.0 miles across the Kaibab Plateau from Point Imperial to the North Kaibab trailhead, surveying cool Canadian Zone forests throughout its length. Only the 3.0-mile segment between Point Imperial and Cape Royal Road follows the plateau rim. This segment of trail maintains mostly gentle grades, alternating from cool, shady conifer forests to openings that afford panoramic vistas into Nankoweap Creek Canyon and beyond. This trip is an excellent choice for a summer day hike when searing heat envelops the Inner Canyon. You need not hike the full 3.0 miles; the first 1.0 mile of trail affords the finest vistas. Walk as far as you wish, find a good viewpoint, then relax and soak in the tremendous panoramas.

Much of the forest along this stretch of the Ken Patrick Trail was consumed by the Outlet Fire in 2000. Although aspen and New Mexican locust are vigorously reclaiming the landscape, there is now less shade along the trail but much better vistas.

The trail begins at the west end of the Point Imperial parking area, the highest point reached by road in Grand Canyon National Park. A series of rock stairs leads you to the trail below, which begins a winding southwest course along the rim. Views from the beginning are dramatic, stretching past the slender Coconino sandstone spire of Mount Hayden into the broad basin of Nankoweap Creek.

Distant features in your view include Marble Canyon, the tortuous gorge of the Little Colorado River, Marble Platform, and the Painted Desert, stretching east to distant mesas that fade away into the desert haze. Even the San Francisco Peaks near Flagstaff are visible on the far southern horizon.

Your view also reaches south along the east rim of the Kaibab Plateau, where dense forest stretches far below onto slopes of the Toroweap and Hermit Formations. An abundance of Rocky Mountain maple on those slopes enlivens the somber forest with crimson foliage in early autumn.

The trail, only occasionally rocky, undulates along the rim for 0.4 mile, passing through a forest of ponderosa pine, Douglas fir, white fir, and aspen. Gambel oak, manzanita, curl-leaf mountain mahogany, and New Mexican locust crowd sunny openings near the rim. After 0.4 mile the trail abruptly descends 120 feet, via moderately steep switchbacks, into the shady confines of a narrow draw just below Point Imperial Road. After reaching the fir- and aspen-shaded floor of the draw, the trail descends briefly through thorny thickets of locust and then begins a steady, moderate ascent away from the road through the cool pine and fir forest to the next high point on the rim.

The pleasant trail next undulates generally southward, rising gently over minor hills and dropping slightly into saddles and shallow draws, staying a short distance west of the rim. En route you capture glimpses into Nankoweap Creek basin and the splintered buttes that punctuate its depths. Views to the northeast begin to open up as you proceed southward along the rim, reaching to Boundary Ridge, Marble Platform, the Echo Cliffs, and distant Navajo Mountain, a broad dome guarding invisible Glen Canyon in southern Utah.

As you gaze southward along the east rim of the plateau, you may notice various features that set this area apart from much of the rest of the Grand Canyon. The Kaibab Formation, which typically forms a broken cliff, has been subdued by erosion here into a steep slope, densely covered with conifer and aspen forest that extends unbroken down to the Coconino sandstone. The east-facing slopes below you receive sunlight only during the morning and early afternoon hours, creating a microclimate that mimics conditions found on the plateau above. You will see tall conifers extending down to the Supai layer and isolated groves that reach down to the base of the Redwall limestone. In most places throughout the Grand Canyon, the Redwall separates

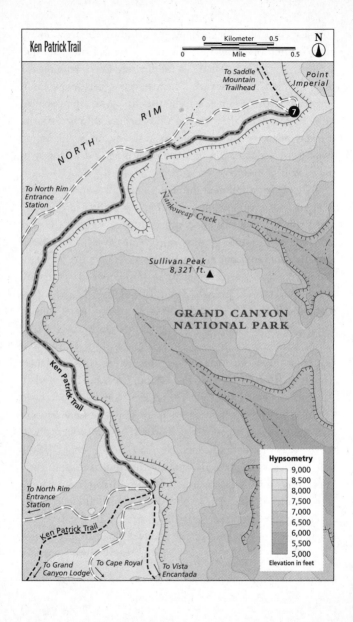

Ken Patrick Trail

NORTH RIM

To Saddle
Mountain
Trailhead

Point
Imperial

7

To North Rim
Entrance
Station

Nankoweap Creek

Sullivan Peak
8,321 ft. ▲

GRAND CANYON
NATIONAL PARK

Ken Patrick Trail

To North Rim
Entrance
Station

Ken Patrick Trail

To Grand
Canyon Lodge

To Cape Royal

To Vista
Encantada

N

0   Kilometer   0.5

0   Mile   0.5

Hypsometry

9,000
8,500
8,000
7,500
7,000
6,500
6,000
5,500
5,000
Elevation in feet

the piñon-juniper woodland above from desert scrub communities below.

After 2.5 miles the trail curves east to the last point affording views into Nankoweap Basin, where a green ribbon of Fremont cottonwoods shades the perennial stream more than 5,000 feet below. From that point, you quickly descend to a saddle, then rise and fall in roller-coaster fashion over two forest-covered hills, finally reaching the rock stairway leading up to the Cape Royal Road at 8,480 feet after 3.0 miles. A seldom-used rim trail continues south for another 3.0 miles to the parking area at Vista Encantada.

If you have not managed to arrange a car shuttle to the two-vehicle turnout 250 yards west of the curve where the trail crosses the road, you will enjoy retracing your view-filled route back to Point Imperial.

Miles and Directions

0.0 Start at the Point Imperial parking area.

3.0 Arrive at Cape Royal Road; turnaround point.

6.0 Arrive back at the Point Imperial parking area.

8 Cape Final

A short but rewarding plateau-top day hike on the North Rim leads to panoramic views.

Distance: 4.0 miles out and back
Hiking time: About 2 hours
Elevation gain: 153 feet
Trail surface: Rehabilitated dirt road; good condition
Water availability: No water available

Best season: Mid-May through mid-Oct
Canine compatibility: Dogs not permitted
Maps: *USGS Walhalla Plateau; Trails Illustrated Grand Canyon National Park*

Finding the trailhead: From the North Rim Entrance Station, proceed into the park for 9.5 miles to the junction with Cape Royal/Point Imperial Road. Turn left and follow the narrow, winding pavement for 5.4 miles to the Y junction with Cape Royal Road, then bear right toward Cape Royal. You pass the crossing of the Ken Patrick Trail after 1.0 mile and the Vista Encantada overlook after 4.6 miles. The small, easy-to-miss Cape Final trailhead, signed "Cape Final Trail Parking," lies on the left (east) side of the road 11.8 miles from the Y junction with Point Imperial Road and 2.5 miles north of the road's end at Cape Royal. GPS N36 8.75' / W111 56.13'

The Hike

This trail offers the greatest rewards for the smallest investment of time and effort of any of the North Rim's plateau-top trails. The route follows a gently rising, long-closed road through parklike forests of ponderosa pine to a panoramic viewpoint on the east rim of the Kaibab Plateau, affording an unusual perspective from high above Unkar Creek Canyon. This leisurely day hike is particularly attractive when summer heat grips the Inner Canyon.

From the trailhead follow the signed Cape Final Trail—actually a long-closed road open to hikers only—east into the open forest of ponderosa pine. The trail rises gently and moderately to the crest of an 8,000-foot ridge after 0.75 mile, then follows an undulating course for another 0.5 mile through peaceful forest to a clearing at the rim of the plateau, where a dramatic view suddenly unfolds.

The depths of Chuar Valley spread out far below. Its broad lower reaches, where hills and gentle slopes are composed of soft Galeros Formation rocks (part of the Precambrian Grand Canyon Supergroup), contrast with the angular profile of the soaring cliffs above. Lava Creek, Chuar's western tributary, is bounded by a striking array of colorful buttes, including the square-edged crag of 7,914-foot Siegfried Pyre and the red Supai-capped Gunther Castle. The deep, serpentine gorge of the Little Colorado River opens up beyond Marble Platform in the southeast, slicing through the platform into the distance.

From the first overlook the trail bends southeast, where piñons begin to supplant the ponderosa pines. The piñons, along with Gambel oak, sagebrush, cliffrose, and curl-leaf mountain mahogany, signal your approach to the rim, where an increase in available sunlight, thin soils, high evaporation, and hot, dry updrafts from the Grand Canyon below create an environment inhospitable to ponderosa pine.

Soon the trail, more apparently an old road, curves back to the south and finally winds its way up between piñon pines to the rocky outcrop of Cape Final. A few tent sites lie on the left side of the trail as it climbs toward the overlook of Cape Final. Because it projects well into the void, it affords

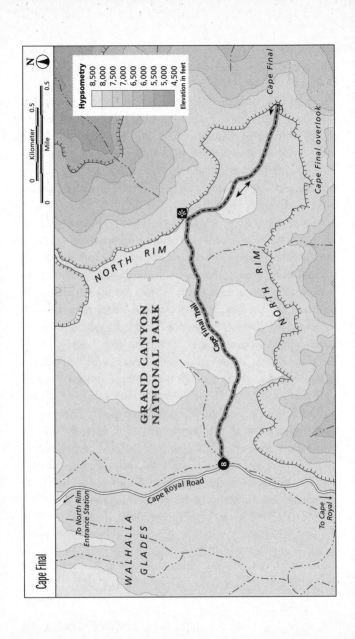

Cape Final

GRAND CANYON NATIONAL PARK

NORTH RIM

NORTH RIM

NORTH RIM

Cape Final Trail

Cape Final

Cape Final overlook

WALHALLA
GLADES

Cape Royal Road

To North Rim
Entrance Station

To Cape
Royal

Hypsometry
8,500
8,000
7,500
7,000
6,500
6,000
5,500
5,000
4,500

Elevation in feet

N

0   Kilometer   0.5

0   Mile   0.5

an all-encompassing view of lower Marble Canyon and the eastern Grand Canyon. Far below lies Unkar Creek, with the bold pyramid of Vishnu Temple as a backdrop, winding through its cliff-bound canyon to broad Unkar Delta at the Colorado River. There the river silently flows through a comparatively wide valley, where long slopes of soft, red Dox sandstone spread out on both sides of the river. Unkar Delta is notable not only for its size—some 300 acres—but also for the number of Ancestral Puebloan dwelling sites discovered there by archaeologists. At least ninety-four sites, many with large rooms and some featuring kivas, suggest Ancestral Puebloans' occupation of Unkar Delta until the late twelfth century.

The vista encompasses a broad sweep of Grand Canyon landscapes. In the southeast your view reaches well into the shadowed gorge of the Little Colorado River and to the towering walls of the Palisades of the Desert, with the rolling hills of the Painted Desert stretching far into the distance beyond. Far to the south rises the Grand Canyon's South Rim, incised by a multitude of steep, short canyons plunging into the Colorado River gorge. Beyond the South Rim, the wooded expanse of the Coconino Plateau reaches out to the San Francisco volcanic field, punctuated by its namesake peaks, and to other lofty cones, such as Kendrick Peak and Bill Williams Mountain.

After enjoying this brief but rewarding hike, retrace your steps to the trailhead.

Miles and Directions

0.0 Start at the Cape Final trailhead.

2.0 Cape Final overlook.

4.0 Arrive back at the Cape Final trailhead.

⑨ Cliff Springs

A short but fascinating walk travels below the rim of Walhalla Plateau.

Distance: 1.0 to 2.0 miles out and back
Hiking time: About 30 minutes to 1 hour
Elevation gain: 250 feet
Trail surface: Unmaintained; good condition
Water availability: Water at Cliff Springs requires treatment; bring your own.

Best season: Mid-May through mid-Oct
Canine compatibility: Dogs not permitted
Maps: USGS *Walhalla Plateau*; Trails Illustrated *Grand Canyon National Park*

Finding the trailhead: From the North Rim Entrance Station, proceed into the park for 9.5 miles to the junction with Cape Royal/ Point Imperial Road. Turn left and follow the narrow, winding pavement for 5.4 miles to the Y junction with Cape Royal Road, then bear right toward Cape Royal. Continue on Cape Royal Road for 13.7 miles to the signed Cliff Springs trailhead, on the left (east) side of the road at Angels Window overlook. The trailhead lies 0.6 mile north of the road's end at Cape Royal. GPS N36 7.48' / W111 56.87'

The Hike

This trail is a fine, albeit brief, introduction to the plateau and rim environments of the North Rim. Distant views, a well-preserved Ancestral Puebloan granary, and a dripping spring hidden in an alcove beneath the rim offer rewarding diversions for visitors budgeting their time and energy.

The brief stroll gets under way at the Angels Window overlook, which affords a fine view of that interesting natural opening in the Kaibab Formation on the east rim of Cape Royal. Carefully cross the busy roadway and follow the wide gravel trail west down a shallow draw through the open forest of ponderosa pine. After only 100 yards you reach the ruins of a well-preserved Ancestral Puebloan granary, hidden beneath a large Kaibab Formation boulder. The Kayenta Ancestral Puebloans who inhabited the Grand Canyon from a.d. 900 to a.d. 1150 were limited in numbers by the scant availability of water and arable land. Living in small bands, these people farmed in the canyons and atop the plateaus of the North Rim and stored their corn, beans, and squash in granaries such as this one.

Stroll down the draw beyond the ruin, descending a moderate grade into a larger draw joining on your right (north). Here Douglas firs join the forest of ponderosa pine, and Gambel oaks gather in ranks on the slopes above. You soon cross the dry, rocky wash on the floor of the draw beneath spreading branches of box elder, then follow a red ledge of Toroweap Formation rocks west. Walls of Kaibab Formation rocks overhang the ledge as you contour above the increasingly deep and rugged draw.

Seeps begin to emerge from the base of the Kaibab cliff, nurturing small clumps of mosses. Within moments you reach a deeper alcove where Cliff Springs emerges. Much like Dripping Springs on the South Rim, numerous seeps converge here and drip steadily into shallow, mossy pools. Fine views, framed by scattered pines and Douglas firs, stretch southeast down the precipitous Clear Creek tributary below, past the erosion-isolated mesa of Wotans Throne to Kendrick Mountain and the San Francisco Peaks, nearly 60 miles distant.

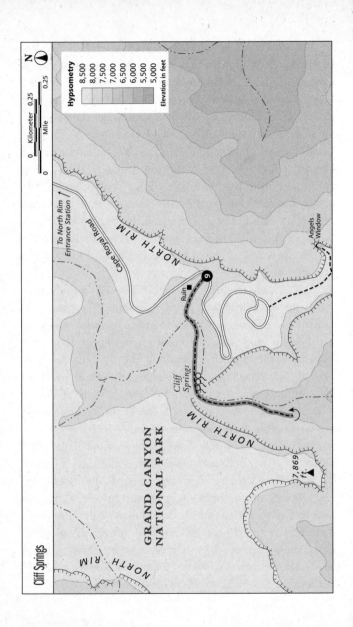

Cliff Springs

GRAND CANYON
NATIONAL PARK

Cape Royal Road

To North Rim
Entrance Station

NORTH RIM

Ruin

Cliff
Springs

NORTH RIM

7,869
ft.

NORTH RIM

Angels
Window

Hypsometry

8,500
8,000
7,500
7,000
6,500
6,000
5,500
5,000

Elevation in feet

N

0   Kilometer 0.25

0   0.25
        Mile

9

The trail continues beyond the springs for 0.5 mile, offering a sampling of the nature of Inner Canyon trails. The route beyond the springs is rough and rocky, undulating over and around obstacles such as boulders and trees. The trail follows the Toroweap Formation ledge past another dripping spring, then bends south and descends along the western flanks of the plummeting canyon below. Here you may notice a change in the environment, since piñon, agave, Utah serviceberry, Mormon tea, and roundleaf buffaloberry have supplanted the conifer forest due to the thin soils, southern exposure, and hot, dry updrafts from the Canyon far below.

The Cape Royal peninsula rises boldly beyond the precipitous canyon to the southeast, bounded by cliffs of the Kaibab Formation and the buff-toned Coconino sandstone, its cross-bedding preserving the great dunes of a vast desert that covered the region 270 million years ago. Vishnu Temple's pyramidal spire juts skyward above the Grand Canyon's vast gulf, beyond the narrow isthmus separating Cape Royal from Wotans Throne.

The trail ends in a shady slickrock alcove surrounded by red Toroweap Formation rocks. Don't attempt to follow the slickrock ledge around the point ahead—sheer cliffs plunge 1,000 feet. Be content with the view from the trail's end and then backtrack to the trailhead.

Miles and Directions

- **0.0** Start at the Cliff Springs trailhead.
- **0.5** Pass Cliff Springs. (**Option:** Turn around here for a 1.0-mile round-trip.)
- **1.0** End of trail; turnaround point.
- **2.0** Arrive back at the Cliff Springs trailhead.

10 Cape Royal

A short, easy walk leads to one of the North Rim's finest vistas.

Distance: 0.8 mile out and back
Hiking time: About 30 minutes
Elevation gain: 165 feet
Trail surface: Paved trail
Water availability: No water available

Best season: Mid-May through mid-Oct
Canine compatibility: Dogs not permitted
Maps: *USGS Cape Royal; Trails Illustrated Grand Canyon National Park*

Finding the trailhead: From the North Rim Entrance Station, proceed into the park for 9.5 miles to the junction with Cape Royal/Point Imperial Road. Turn left and follow the narrow, winding pavement for 5.4 miles to the Y junction with Cape Royal Road, then bear right toward Cape Royal. Continue on Cape Royal Road for 14.3 miles to the end of the road at Cape Royal. Look for pit toilets and a picnic site at the parking area. GPS N36 7.34' / W 111 56.97'

The Hike

The promontory of Cape Royal, jutting southward into the Grand Canyon away from the North Rim, is a prominent landmark seen from many South Rim viewpoints. The point affords one of the Canyon's more memorable vistas, and it is one of only two points on the North Rim offering views of the Colorado River. If you have only one day to spend on the North Rim, the short walk to Cape Royal should be at the top of your "must-do" list.

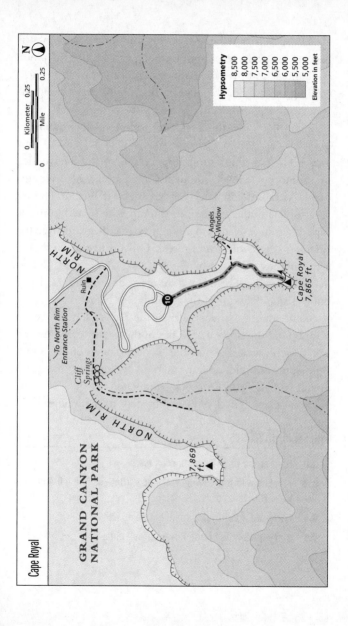

Cape Royal

GRAND CANYON
NATIONAL PARK

NORTH RIM

7,869 ft. ▲

Cliff Springs

To North Rim Entrance Station ←

NORTH RIM

Ruin

10

Angels Window

Cape Royal
7,865 ft. ▲

N

0   Kilometer   0.25
0   Mile   0.25

Hypsometry

8,500
8,000
7,500
7,000
6,500
6,000
5,500
5,000

Elevation in feet

The paved trail begins at the southeast corner of the parking area and leads south among a scattering of piñon and juniper and over the light-gray Kaibab Formation rocks capping this part of the plateau. Interpretive signs along the way offer insights into the natural history of the area.

After 0.2 mile the 150-yard path to Angels Window branches left, leading to one of the Grand Canyon's few arches. The trail ahead soon drops off the level of the wooded promontory to the viewpoint at Cape Royal, where a memorable vista unfolds. The wooded mesa of Wotans Throne, an erosional outlier of the North Rim, is separated from the cape by a knife-blade ridge. Its mesa stands guard over the yawning depths of Vishnu Creek Canyon to the south and a precipitous tributary of Clear Creek to the west. Vishnu Temple, Krishna Shrine, and an array of colorful, castlelike buttes rise boldly out of the great depths below.

Cliff bands of the Palisades of the Desert and the South Rim bound the opposite reaches of the Grand Canyon from east to southwest. Beyond the wooded fringe of the South Rim, some 60 miles distant, rise the lofty summits of the San Francisco Peaks and Kendrick Mountain.

From Cape Royal, retrace your steps to the trailhead.

Miles and Directions

0.0 Start at the Cape Royal parking area.

0.2 Junction with trail to Angels Window. (**Option:** Turn left and walk 150 yards to Angels Window.)

0.4 Arrive at Cape Royal; turnaround point.

0.8 Arrive back at the Cape Royal parking area.

11 Widforss Trail

A plateau-top half-day hike follows a self-guided nature trail on the North Rim.

Distance: 4.2 miles out and back
Hiking time: About 2 to 2.5 hours
Elevation gain: 170 feet
Trail surface: Unmaintained; good condition
Water availability: No water available

Best season: Mid-May through mid-Oct
Canine compatibility: Dogs not permitted
Maps: *USGS Bright Angel Point; Trails Illustrated Grand Canyon National Park; Earthwalk Grand Canyon National Park*

Finding the trailhead: From the North Rim Entrance Station, proceed into the park for 9.5 miles to the Cape Royal/Point Imperial Road junction and continue straight ahead; the sign points to "Visitor Services." You reach a sign showing the turnoff to Widforss Point after another 0.25 mile. Turn right here onto a good gravel road and skirt the margins of Harvey Meadow for another 0.6 mile to the signed trailhead on the left (west) side of the road. GPS N36 13.42' / W11 3.90'

The Hike

The Widforss Trail is arguably the finest plateau-top trail in Grand Canyon National Park. The route hugs the rim of The Transept, an abysmal tributary of Bright Angel Creek, as it passes splendid Grand Canyon viewpoints between shady stands of conifer and aspen. The mildly undulating trail is well defined and easy to follow throughout its length. No water is available en route; be sure to pack an ample supply.

The trail and a point on the North Rim were named in honor of the artist Gunnar M. Widforss, the "painter of the national parks." Widforss spent much time in the 1920s and 1930s creating vivid watercolor images of the Grand Canyon, his favorite national park. Fourteen numbered posts along the first 2.1 miles of the trail are keyed to a pamphlet available from a dispenser at the trailhead. Pick one up before heading out on the trail; it will enhance your enjoyment and understanding through insight into some of the natural features and processes found along the trail.

The trail begins along the fringes of Harvey Meadow, heading south among scattered groves of Engelmann spruce, white fir, ponderosa pine, and aspen. A pair of rocky switchbacks soon lead up and over exposures of Kaibab Formation rocks to the beginning of a lengthy traverse high above The Transept, a 4,000-foot-deep tributary canyon of Bright Angel Creek. François Matthes, a topographer with the US Geological Survey, declared in the early 1900s that The Transept was far grander than Yosemite Valley. Although you may not agree, The Transept is an impressive defile nonetheless.

The trail bends in and out of seven minor draws, staying just north of the rim during the first 2.2 miles. At first you proceed above the headwaters draw of The Transept, where you can see a dense forest of spire-topped spruce and fir, reminiscent of a subalpine forest in the Rocky Mountains, on the north-facing slopes above it. Soon that draw begins to plummet away into the gaping abyss of The Transept, as the trail proceeds west along the rim through a forest of ponderosa pine, white fir, and aspen. Engelmann spruce joins the forest only in the shadiest draws.

Typical of most rim trails, the route often stays away from the rim. Rather than a continuum of Grand Canyon vistas,

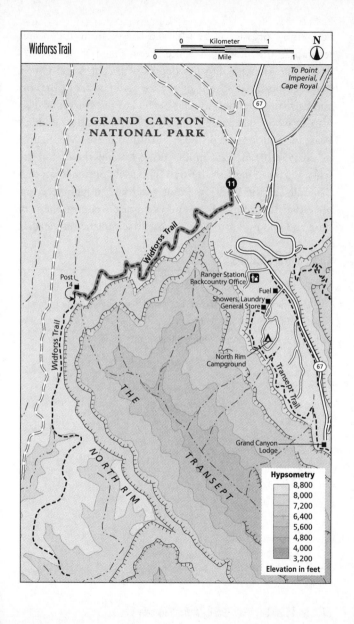

Widforss Trail

GRAND CANYON
NATIONAL PARK

To Point
Imperial,
Cape Royal

67

11

Widforss Trail

Post
14

Widforss Trail

Ranger Station
Backcountry Office

Fuel

Showers, Laundry
General Store

North Rim
Campground

Transept Trail

67

Grand Canyon
Lodge

THE

NORTH

RIM

TRANSEPT

Hypsometry	
	8,800
	8,000
	7,200
	6,400
	5,600
	4,800
	4,000
	3,200

Elevation in feet

Kilometer

Mile

N

you enjoy occasional tree-framed views from the points separating the draws en route. Long-range views extend down The Transept into the depths of Bright Angel Creek, bounded on the southeast by the towering buttes of Brahma and Zoroaster Temples, and far beyond to the Coconino Plateau, its wooded expanse punctuated by Red Butte, Kendrick Peak, the San Francisco Peaks, and Bill Williams Mountain.

At Post 14, after 2.1 miles, you've reached the end of the self-guided segment of the trail. The trail continues another 2.8 miles to the Widforss Point overlook, though to complete that rewarding hike requires a greater commitment of time and energy. From Post 14, backtrack to the trailhead.

Miles and Directions

0.0 Start at the Widforss trailhead.

2.1 Arrive at Post 14, the end of the self-guiding segment of the trail; turnaround point.

4.2 Arrive back at the Widforss trailhead.

12 Uncle Jim Trail

A plateau-top hike reaches a viewpoint on the North Rim.

Distance: 3.9-mile lollipop
Hiking time: About 2 to 3 hours
Elevation gain: 200 feet
Trail surface: Unmaintained; good condition
Water availability: No water available
Best season: Mid-May through mid-Oct

Other trail users: Mules
Canine compatibility: Dogs not permitted
Maps: *USGS Bright Angel Point; Trails Illustrated Grand Canyon National Park; Earthwalk Grand Canyon National Park or Bright Angel Trail*

Finding the trailhead: From Jacob Lake, follow AZ 67 south for 31.2 miles to the North Rim Entrance Station, then continue south into the park. The park highway ahead winds through lovely meadows and forests of pine, fir, spruce, and aspen. You pass the Cape Royal/Point Imperial Road junction after 9.5 miles. Continue straight ahead for another 0.9 mile, where a prominent sign indicates the Kaibab Trail parking lot on the left (east) side of the road.

This parking lot fills to capacity nearly every day by late morning. If it is full when you arrive, you must drive to the public parking areas near Grand Canyon Lodge and then either walk the mule trail that parallels the park road for 1.5 miles to the trailhead or ride the shuttle bus. (Inquire at the Grand Canyon Lodge transportation desk for shuttle schedules.) GPS N36 13.07' / W 112 3.36'

The Hike

The mildly undulating Uncle Jim Trail traverses cool Kaibab Plateau forests en route to a splendid Grand Canyon viewpoint. From trail's end, hikers gain an excellent overview of

Roaring Springs Canyon and can visually trace the route of the North Kaibab Trail as it winds its way from the North Rim to the Redwall limestone.

The trail, waterless throughout its length, is rougher and rockier than other North Rim trails due to occasional mule traffic. Overnight camping is allowed on this route (with a backcountry use permit), making it a good choice for a short backpack when intense summer heat grips the Inner Grand Canyon. Most hikers can complete this hike in about two hours, but three hours allows for a more leisurely pace.

The trail was named in honor of James T. "Uncle Jim" Owens. Formerly a game warden in Yellowstone National Park, Owens was hired in 1906 by the Forest Service to serve as game warden in the Grand Canyon Game Reserve on the Kaibab Plateau. He lived part-time in the cave near the Widforss trailhead on the north edge of Harvey Meadow. At the time, game management theories called for the elimination of "undesirable" predatory species in favor of "harmless" wildlife such as deer. By 1918 Uncle Jim claimed to have killed 532 mountain lions. The tragic result was the explosive growth of the Kaibab deer population, reaching an estimated 100,000 deer by 1924. The population was far greater than their limited range on the Kaibab Plateau could sustain, and thousands died of starvation during the hard winter of 1924–25. Today we recognize that predators are more efficient game managers, and mountain lions now thrive on the Kaibab Plateau.

Uncle Jim Owens did leave a better legacy to the Grand Canyon region. In 1906 he and others brought bison to the Kaibab Plateau. This herd was the progenitor of the herd that now occupies the House Rock Valley.

The Uncle Jim and Ken Patrick Trails begin as a single path from the east edge of the North Kaibab trailhead parking lot adjacent to the mule corral. At first the trails follow the North Rim east through a forest of ponderosa pine and aspen. The trees' ranks open enough to afford fine views into the rugged depths of Roaring Springs Canyon and, beyond, the South Rim and the distant San Francisco Peaks.

Soon you contour away from the rim, entering heavy forest dominated by white fir. The previously level trail dips into a minor draw, then gradually ascends to a signed junction at 8,300 feet beneath a grove of stout, towering pines. Bear right here onto the Uncle Jim Trail. The tread becomes quite gravelly ahead as you descend a moderate grade northeast through mixed conifer forest into the shady confines of the headwaters draw of Roaring Springs Canyon. As you ascend a moderate grade out of the draw, Engelmann spruce makes a brief appearance among the pine, fir, and aspen on the sheltered northwest-facing slopes.

After ascending a few minor switchbacks, you then rise to an unsigned junction at 8,350 feet, where you are faced with the only decision you must make on this trip. This junction marks the beginning of a loop trail to Uncle Jim Point. Both legs of the loop reach the point and are about 1.0 mile long, but since the left leg leads to Grand Canyon views sooner, most hikers bear left at the junction. That leg of the loop ascends gently through peaceful forest.

After 0.3 mile you gain the top of a broad ridge at your high point of 8,427 feet and then begin a long curve toward the south. The trail skirts the east rim of the ridge, where views open up into the cliff-bound depths of upper Bright Angel Canyon and beyond to the flat, forested expanse of

Walhalla Plateau. These features soon fade from view as you duck back into the forest and head away from the rim.

About 1.1 miles from the loop trail junction, you meet the west leg of the loop joining from the north. Continue straight ahead, past a dilapidated mule hitching rail, and follow the path down over slabs of Kaibab Formation rocks out to the overlook, just below the rim at 8,300 feet. Here the rim effect is well pronounced. Piñon, juniper, cliffrose, and Utah serviceberry from the Inner Canyon share space with Gambel oak, ponderosa pine, and white fir, trees of the Kaibab Plateau high country.

Though your view is somewhat obstructed by the small trees and shrubs massed at the point, it reaches far below into the abyss of Roaring Springs Canyon, past its confluence with Bright Angel Canyon, to a high ridge capped by bold towers: Deva Temple, Hattan Butte, and Brahma and Zoroaster Temples. The long-range view stretches 12 miles across the Grand Canyon to the South Rim and beyond. Look out across the thickly wooded expanse of the Coconino Plateau, punctuated by the summits of Red Butte near the town of Tusayan; 9,256-foot Bill Williams Mountain; 10,418-foot Kendrick Peak; and the lofty San Francisco Peaks. The view is crowned by 12,633-foot Humphreys Peak, the highest point in Arizona.

The well-defined switchbacks of the North Kaibab Trail can be seen leading through the cliffs into Roaring Springs Canyon, and you can visually trace that trail through the Redwall limestone into Bright Angel Canyon far below. To return to the trailhead, backtrack several yards to the junction and bear left onto the west leg of the loop. This pleasant but viewless trail mildly undulates through a forest of white fir, ponderosa pine, and aspen for 1.0 mile to the junction with

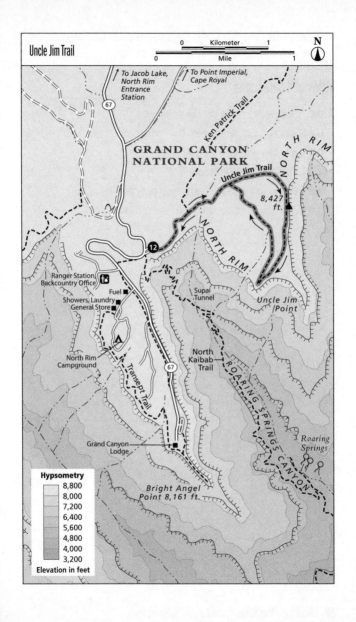

Uncle Jim Trail

0   Kilometer   1

0   Mile   1

N

To Jacob Lake,
North Rim
Entrance
Station

To Point Imperial,
Cape Royal

67

Ken Patrick Trail

**GRAND CANYON
NATIONAL PARK**

NORTH RIM

Uncle Jim Trail

8,427
ft.

NORTH RIM

12

Uncle Jim
Point

Ranger Station
Backcountry Office

Fuel

Showers, Laundry
General Store

Supai
Tunnel

North Rim
Campground

North
Kaibab
Trail

Transept Trail

67

ROARING SPRINGS CANYON

Grand Canyon
Lodge

Roaring
Springs

Hypsometry

8,800
8,000
7,200
6,400
5,600
4,800
4,000
3,200

Elevation in feet

Bright Angel
Point 8,161 ft.

the other leg of the loop. Bear left there and retrace your steps for 0.9 mile to the trailhead.

Miles and Directions

0.0 Start at the North Kaibab trailhead.

0.4 Junction with Ken Patrick Trail; bear right.

0.9 Junction with loop trail; bear left.

2.0 Pass Uncle Jim Point overlook.

3.0 Return to the junction with loop trail; bear left.

3.9 Arrive back at the North Kaibab trailhead.

13 North Kaibab Trail to Supai Tunnel

A half-day out-and-back hike traverses below the rim on the North Rim's only maintained Inner Canyon trail.

Distance: 3.6 miles out and back
Hiking time: About 3 to 4 hours
Elevation gain: 1,410 feet
Trail surface: Maintained; excellent condition
Water availability: Piped water is available May through Oct at Supai Tunnel. Always bring your own in the event of a pipeline break.

Best season: Mid-May through mid-Oct
Other trail users: Mules
Canine compatibility: Dogs not permitted
Maps: *USGS Bright Angel Point; Trails Illustrated Grand Canyon National Park; Earthwalk Bright Angel Trail or Grand Canyon National Park*

Finding the trailhead: From Jacob Lake follow AZ 67 south for 31.2 miles to the North Rim Entrance Station. Continue into the park 9.5 miles to the Cape Royal/Point Imperial Road junction. Continue straight ahead for another 0.9 mile, where a prominent sign indicates the Kaibab Trail parking lot to the left (east) side of the road.

This parking lot fills to capacity nearly every day by late morning. If it is full when you arrive, you must drive to the public parking areas near Grand Canyon Lodge and then either walk the mule trail that parallels the park road for 1.5 miles to the trailhead or ride the shuttle bus. (Inquire at the Grand Canyon Lodge transportation desk for shuttle schedules.) GPS N36 13.03' / W112 3.40'

The Hike

The North Kaibab Trail is the North Rim's only maintained trail, lying within the frequently patrolled trans-canyon

Corridor Zone of the park. Unlike many of the Grand Canyon's trails, which follow the path of least resistance in search of breaks in the cliff bands, this straightforward trail forges its way through obstructions. More hikers pound this trail than any other on the North Rim, for ample reasons. The tread is wide and only occasionally rocky, and it descends moderately rather than steeply. The way offers a classic sampling of all the life zones present in the Grand Canyon, and the landscapes it traverses and views it affords are dramatic.

The 3.6-mile round-trip to Supai Tunnel offers memorable Inner Canyon views and a fine introduction to Grand Canyon hiking. The high elevations that the trail traverses are cooler in summer than other Inner Canyon trails, though temperatures can still be hot. A fine alternative to hiking all the way to Supai Tunnel is the 1.4-mile round-trip to the ledges atop the Coconino sandstone, only 500 feet below the rim. The top of the Coconino affords unobstructed views into the yawning depths of Roaring Springs Canyon.

The North Kaibab Trail is used by day riders on mule trains to Supai Tunnel and Roaring Springs. If you encounter a mule train, step quietly to the side of the trail and follow the wrangler's instructions.

The trail begins behind the information sign at the rim, below the entrance to the trailhead parking lot. You descend steadily at once, passing through a cool forest of white fir, Douglas fir, ponderosa pine, and aspen. The initial descent through Kaibab Formation rocks passes unnoticed, since erosion has subdued the Kaibab's typical cliff into a slope cloaked behind dense vegetation. Switchbacks soon lead you deeper into the void of Roaring Springs Canyon, and the grade abates briefly atop sheer, desert-varnished cliffs of Coconino sandstone. Gnarled pines and firs clinging to the

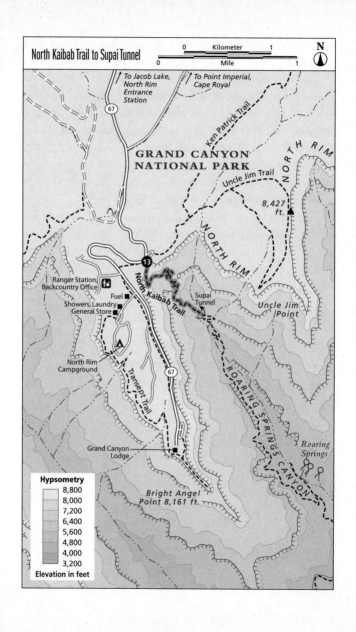

North Kaibab Trail to Supai Tunnel

Kilometer 0 — 1
Mile 0 — 1

N

To Jacob Lake,
North Rim
Entrance
Station

To Point Imperial,
Cape Royal

67

Ken Patrick Trail

GRAND CANYON
NATIONAL PARK

Uncle Jim Trail

8,427
ft.

NORTH RIM

NORTH RIM

Ranger Station,
Backcountry Office

13

North Kaibab Trail

Supai Tunnel

Uncle Jim
Point

Fuel

Showers, Laundry
General Store

North Rim
Campground

Transept Trail

67

ROARING SPRINGS CANYON

Grand Canyon
Lodge

Roaring
Springs

Bright Angel
Point 8,161 ft.

Hypsometry

8,800
8,000
7,200
6,400
5,600
4,800
4,000
3,200

Elevation in feet

slickrock rim of the cliffs are reminiscent of a scene from Yosemite.

Conifers persist as you follow switchbacks through the break in the Coconino. A wide variety of shrubs dress these slopes and the red slopes of Hermit Formation rocks below. En route the trail forges a way through thickets of Rocky Mountain maple, Gambel oak, mallow ninebark, elderberry, thorny New Mexican locust, wild rose, and silk-tassel. An occasional juniper infiltrates the ranks of Douglas fir and white fir that dominate the shady slopes.

After 1.8 miles (at 6,840 feet), you reach a water faucet offering seasonal water and toilets in a confined rocky draw. Just ahead at the portal of Supai Tunnel is a passageway through the Esplanade sandstone. From the confines of the shady draw, retrace your steps to the trailhead.

Miles and Directions

0.0 Start at the North Kaibab trailhead.

1.8 Arrive at Supai Tunnel; turnaround point.

3.6 Arrive back at the North Kaibab trailhead.

14 Transept Trail

A pleasant one-way or out-and-back walk travels through the forest along the North Rim.

Distance: 1.7-mile shuttle; 3.4 miles out and back

Hiking time: About 45 minutes to 1 hour one-way; 1.5 to 2 hours round-trip

Elevation loss: 100 feet

Trail surface: Unmaintained; good condition

Water availability: Available at the campground and the lodge

Best season: Mid-May through mid-Oct

Canine compatibility: Leashed dogs permitted

Maps: *USGS Bright Angel Point; Trails Illustrated Grand Canyon National Park; Earthwalk Bright Angel Trail or Grand Canyon National Park*

Finding the trailhead: From Jacob Lake follow AZ 67 south for 31.2 miles to the North Rim Entrance Station. Continue into the park 9.5 miles to the Cape Royal/Point Imperial Road junction. Continue straight ahead for another 0.9 mile, where a prominent sign indicates the Kaibab Trail. Continue straight ahead along the primary park road for another 2.3 miles to the spacious public parking lots located on the left (east) side of the road just before it ends at Grand Canyon Lodge.

To leave a shuttle car at North Rim Campground, turn right at the prominently signed campground road 1.2 miles north of the lodge (or 11.5 miles south of the North Rim Entrance Station) and drive 0.3 mile to the campground. The trail is next to the general store near the campground entrance. Spur trails also connect the campground with the Transept Trail. Grand Canyon Lodge GPS N36 11.82' / W112 3.20'

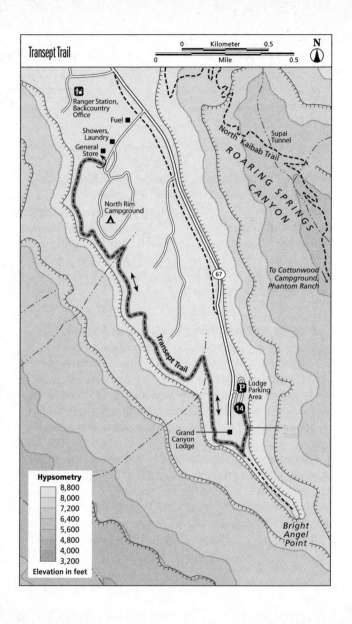

Transept Trail

Kilometer 0.5
Mile 0.5

N

Ranger Station,
Backcountry
Office

Fuel

Showers,
Laundry

General Store

North Rim
Campground

North Kaibab Trail

ROARING SPRINGS CANYON

Supai
Tunnel

67

To Cottonwood
Campground,
Phantom Ranch

Transept Trail

Lodge
Parking
Area

14

Grand
Canyon
Lodge

Bright
Angel
Point

Hypsometry

8,800
8,000
7,200
6,400
5,600
4,800
4,000
3,200

Elevation in feet

The Hike

This trail is most frequently used by campground guests as a connector from North Rim Campground to Grand Canyon Lodge. Day hikers can use the trail, but they must park in the public parking lots at the lodge. From there find the trail by following the Bright Angel Point Trail to the lodge and turning right, or simply walk through the lodge and find the trail below the patio.

The Transept Trail is smooth and generally level, except for a 100-foot descent (or ascent, depending on your direction of travel) in the first 0.4 mile from the campground. The trail passes through cool forests of pine, fir, and aspen as it bends into four minor draws along the rim of The Transept, a prominent tributary canyon of Bright Angel Creek. Due to moderate forest cover, hikers will enjoy only occasional glimpses into the 3,200-foot-deep trench of The Transept.

Miles and Directions

0.0 Start at Grand Canyon Lodge.

1.7 Arrive at North Rim Campground. End your hike here if you've arranged a shuttle, or turn around and retrace your steps.

3.4 Arrive back at Grand Canyon Lodge.

15 Bright Angel Point

A short out-and-back walk leads to a dramatic vista point on the North Rim.

Distance: 0.8 mile out and back
Hiking time: About 30 minutes
Elevation gain: 90 feet
Trail surface: Paved trail
Water availability: Available at Grand Canyon Lodge
Best season: Mid-May through mid-Oct

Canine compatibility: Dogs not permitted
Maps: *USGS Bright Angel Point; Trails Illustrated Grand Canyon National Park; Earthwalk Bright Angel Trail or Grand Canyon National Park*

Finding the trailhead: From Jacob Lake follow AZ 67 south for 31.2 miles to the North Rim Entrance Station. Continue into the park 9.5 miles to the Cape Royal/Point Imperial Road junction. Continue straight ahead for another 0.9 mile, where a prominent sign indicates the Kaibab Trail. Continue straight ahead along the primary park road for another 2.3 miles to the spacious public parking lots located on the left (east) side of the road just before it ends at Grand Canyon Lodge. GPS N36 11.91' / W112 3.13'

The Hike

Grand Canyon Lodge, at road's end on the North Rim, is the focal point for the majority of visitors to this remote part of Grand Canyon National Park. While you're here enjoying the comforts of the lodge or simply visiting for the day, don't miss the short and easy stroll to Bright Angel Point, an overlook that affords one of the most dramatic views of the

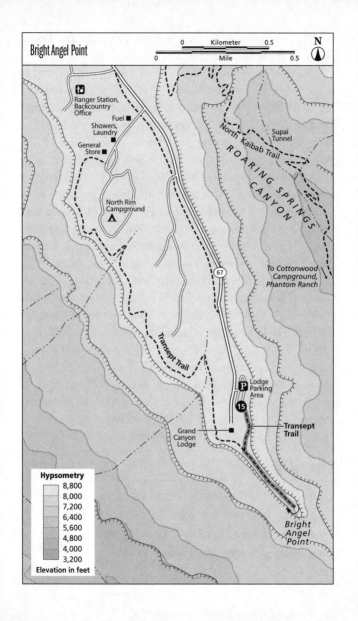

Bright Angel Point

Ranger Station,
Backcountry
Office

Fuel ■

Showers,
Laundry ■

General Store ■

North Rim
Campground

Transept Trail

North Kaibab Trail

Supai
Tunnel

ROARING SPRINGS CANYON

67

To Cottonwood
Campground,
Phantom Ranch

Lodge
Parking
Area

15

Grand
Canyon
Lodge

Transept
Trail

Bright
Angel
Point

Kilometer

Mile

N

Hypsometry

8,800
8,000
7,200
6,400
5,600
4,800
4,000
3,200

Elevation in feet

Grand Canyon from the North Rim. There are few better places to enjoy an incomparable Canyon sunrise or sunset.

Day-use visitors will find the trail behind the log shelter at the public parking lot. Guests staying at the lodge can find the trail below the east patio behind the lodge. Pamphlets describing this self-guided nature trail are available from the dispenser at the log shelter.

From the public parking lot, follow the trail as it leads south between the rim of Roaring Springs Canyon and the lodge cabins. After 250 yards the trail from the lodge joins on your right (0.1 mile from the lodge itself). The trail ahead follows the crest of a narrow Kaibab Formation promontory among scattered piñon and juniper for another 0.3 mile to the 8,150-foot viewpoint, where a breathtaking vista unfolds.

A score of colorful buttes, the mile-deep trough of the Grand Canyon, and the soaring battlements of the South Rim spread out in an explosion of color and form. The gaping trench of Bright Angel Creek lies virtually at your feet, its bottom 4,000 feet below. You can visually trace that arrow-straight canyon far into the depths of the Grand Canyon and beyond to the South Rim. On the far southern horizon rise the lofty highlands of the San Francisco Peaks, Kendrick Mountain, Red Butte, and Bill Williams Mountain.

From the point, return the way you came.

Miles and Directions

0.0 Start at the Grand Canyon Lodge public parking area.

0.2 Junction with trail from lodge; continue straight ahead.

0.4 Arrive at Bright Angel Point; turnaround point.

0.8 Arrive back at the parking area.

16 North Bass Trail to Muav Cabin

A half-day out-and-back hike travels from a remote North Rim trailhead to a historic cabin below the rim.

Distance: 2.0 miles out and back

Hiking time: About 2.5 hours

Elevation gain: 820 feet

Trail surface: Unmaintained; fair condition

Water availability: No water available

Best season: Late May or early June through mid-Oct

Canine compatibility: Dogs not permitted

Maps: *USGS King Arthur Castle; Trails Illustrated Grand Canyon National Park*

Finding the trailhead: From Jacob Lake follow AZ 67 south for 26.5 miles to the prominently signed junction with FR 22 (also signed for Dry Park 10) and turn right (west). This junction lies 0.9 mile south of Kaibab Lodge and immediately south of tiny Deer Lake. This good gravel road, with washboards, ascends steadily through spruce, fir, and aspen forest for 2.1 miles to the signed junction with FR 270, where you turn left (south). Follow this occasionally rough and rocky road for 2.3 miles, avoiding two unsigned right-forking roads en route, to a junction where a sign points west to Fire Point 12. Turn right here onto FR 223, also rough and rocky in places, and proceed 5.8 miles to left-branching FR 268, signed for Swamp Point, your destination.

Follow FR 268 south; it's rough and rocky in places. After 0.3 mile, turn left onto FR 268B, a good but narrow gravel road. Follow FR 268B for 1.2 miles to the national park boundary, where the road is designated W4 and its condition quickly deteriorates. Rocks, roots, potholes, and, farther on, high centers make the use of a high-clearance vehicle advisable. After driving 0.2 mile from the park boundary, avoid an unsigned road that branches left to Kanabownits Spring. Bear right, proceeding generally west through the pristine forest of pine, fir, and aspen. You will pass an inviting camping/parking area 7.8 miles from the park boundary, after which the road becomes extremely rough and rocky for the final 0.1 mile to the Swamp Point trailhead, 19.6 miles from AZ 67.

Hikers arriving late in the day can camp wherever they wish along the access roads within Kaibab National Forest. You can camp at the Swamp Point trailhead only after obtaining a permit from the Backcountry Information Office (Use Area NJO, Swamp Ridge).

Note: The final segment of the road to Swamp Point within park boundaries is blocked each winter by fallen trees. National Park Service fire crews may not clear the road until mid-June or later each year. Park regulations prohibit driving off established roadways. Consult park rangers regarding road conditions before driving this road. GPS N36 20.14' / W112 21.0'

The Hike

Historic Muav Cabin rests in a pine grove just north of Muav Saddle, a prominent notch separating the North Rim from isolated Powell Plateau. The cabin is easily reached via the best segment of the North Bass Trail, one of the most difficult and demanding trails in the Grand Canyon. This trail, an old Indian route once known as the Shinumo Trail (*shinumo* is a Paiute word referring to the ancient cliff-dwelling inhabitants of the Canyon), was later improved by a prospector known only as White, who may have lived for a time near the spring near Muav Saddle. William Wallace Bass, who constructed the South Bass Trail in the 1880s, rebuilt the so-called White Trail to the North Rim by 1900. Using a cable crossing at the Colorado River, Bass guided tourists from the South Rim to the North Rim via his trail, some on sightseeing trips, others on hunting trips.

Much of the scenery en route is quite different from any other area in the Grand Canyon. Erosion along the Muav

Fault has softened the abrupt edges of the North Rim and upper Muav Canyon, which has a broad, V-shaped profile. Soils in Muav Canyon are well developed, and dense brush forms a perpetually green veneer that masks the broken, rocky slopes.

From road's end at Swamp Point, the trail follows a series of switchbacks on a moderately descending grade via the steep slopes west of the point. Views are excellent from the beginning, stretching northwest across the wooded red-rock platform of The Esplanade into broad Tapeats Amphitheater. The slopes below the point were charred in a 1989 fire. Now, among the blackened snags of piñon and juniper, thickets of Gambel oak, silk-tassel, and Utah serviceberry have reclaimed the slopes.

As the rocky switchbacks lead closer to Muav Saddle, hikers exchange views of Tapeats Amphitheater for views down the deep, brushy trough of Muav Canyon to an array of colorful buttes and the distant South Rim. Muav Cabin comes into view, nestled in a shady grove of ponderosa pines, as you approach the saddle. After 1.0 mile you reach an unmarked junction in the deep notch of Muav Saddle amid a thicket of Gambel oak at 6,711 feet. Trails lead straight ahead to Powell Plateau, right to Muav Cabin, and left to Muav Canyon. Turn right and descend several yards to the cabin.

Muav Cabin, built as a patrol cabin by the National Park Service in 1925, lies several yards north of the saddle via a well-worn path. President Theodore Roosevelt camped near the site while hunting mountain lions in 1903, hence the cabin is sometimes called Teddy's Cabin. The structure, with two rooms and cots, is in remarkably good condition. After contemplating the cabin's history and enjoying the region's quiet beauty, backtrack to the trailhead.

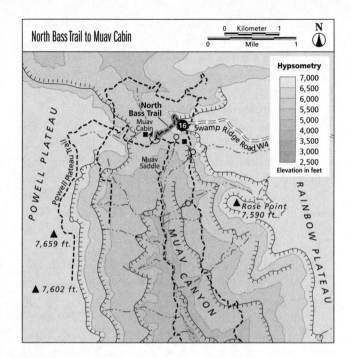

North Bass Trail to Muav Cabin

Hypsometry

7,000
6,500
6,000
5,500
5,000
4,500
4,000
3,500
3,000
2,500
Elevation in feet

POWELL PLATEAU

Powell Plateau Trail

North Bass Trail

Muav Cabin

16 Swamp Ridge Road W4

Muav Saddle

MUAV CANYON

Rose Point 7,590 ft.

RAINBOW PLATEAU

▲ 7,659 ft.

▲ 7,602 ft.

Miles and Directions

0.0 Start at the Swamp Point trailhead.

1.0 Arrive at the trail junction at Muav Saddle; turn right and descend to Muav Cabin; turnaround point.

2.0 Arrive back at the Swamp Point trailhead.

17 Bill Hall Trail to Monument Point

An easy, short out-and-back hike leads to a remote North Rim viewpoint overlooking the central Grand Canyon.

Distance: 1.6 miles out and back

Hiking time: About 1 hour

Elevation gain: 176 feet

Trail surface: Unmaintained; fair to good condition

Water availability: No water available

Best season: Mid-May through mid-Oct

Canine compatibility: Dogs not permitted

Maps: USGS Tapeats Amphitheater; Trails Illustrated Grand Canyon National Park

Finding the trailhead: Although the driving distance to the Bill Hall trailhead is longer than any other in Grand Canyon National Park, the gravel roads are in very good condition. The 1.5-hour trip from the highway is an enjoyable scenic drive through the rich forests of the Kaibab Plateau.

From Jacob Lake follow AZ 67 south for 26.5 miles to the junction with FR 22 (also signed for Dry Park 10) and turn right (west). This junction lies 0.9 mile south of Kaibab Lodge and immediately south of tiny Deer Lake. All junctions ahead are well signed. Stay on FR 22 (sometimes signed FR 422) for 17.6 miles and then turn left onto FR 425, signed for Thunder River Trail 13. After another 7.7 miles, avoid right-branching FR 233 (signed for Wilderness Trails); it leads to trailheads on the fringes of the Kanab Creek Wilderness. After another 0.6 mile, also avoid right-branching FR 232, signed for Thunder River Trail 5, which leads to the Indian Hollow trailhead. Stay left at that junction, remaining on FR 425, signed for Crazy Jug Point 4.

Continue straight for another 1.7 miles (10.0 miles from FR 22), where FR 425 branches left and becomes a poor, unmaintained road at a junction adjacent to the Big Saddle Cabin and corrals. Bear right here, staying on the good gravel road, now FR 292. Bear right again after 0.25 mile and follow signs pointing to Crazy Jug Point. Soon you reach a four-way junction atop the North Rim, 1.5 miles from FR 425. Follow the middle fork (FR 292A), a smooth but narrow dirt road, for the remaining 1.7 miles to the spacious trailhead parking area at road's end, 30.8 miles from the highway.

All roads en route to the trailhead lie within the boundaries of the Kaibab National Forest. Hikers arriving late in the day can camp wherever they wish along the route. GPS N36 27.54' / W112 29.30'

The Hike

This trip combines a satisfying scenic drive through the rich conifer forests of the Kaibab Plateau with a short hike to remote Monument Point. Vistas from the point survey a broad panorama of the central Grand Canyon, a landscape viewed by only a handful of visitors each year, and one far different from more familiar scenes in the eastern Grand Canyon. The trail also passes through the wake of a lightning-caused fire that charred thousands of acres of forest and woodland on the western reaches of the Kaibab Plateau in spring 1996. As early as the fall of that year, grasses were reclaiming the charred ground, and Gambel oaks were vigorously sending out new branches from their root crowns. Charred snags of piñon and juniper remind hikers of the rich woodland that once thrived here—a woodland that will likely take many generations to regenerate.

From the trailhead, pass through a gate in an old fence line. Avoid a right-branching forest road and follow the trail to the left, indicated by National Park Service signs. Within moments the trail leads down to a saddle on the rim, where it forks. The right branch is the main trail; the left branch leads a short distance to a point offering a fine view of Tapeats

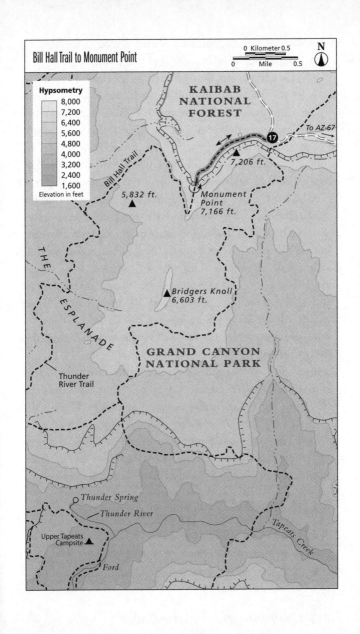

Bill Hall Trail to Monument Point

0 Kilometer 0.5

0 Mile 0.5

N

Hypsometry
8,000
7,200
6,400
5,600
4,800
4,000
3,200
2,400
1,600
Elevation in feet

KAIBAB
NATIONAL
FOREST

To AZ-67

17

7,206 ft.

Bill Hall Trail

5,832 ft.

Monument
Point
7,166 ft.

THE
ESPLANADE

Bridgers Knoll
6,603 ft.

GRAND CANYON
NATIONAL PARK

Thunder
River Trail

Thunder Spring
Thunder River

Tapeats Creek

Upper Tapeats
Campsite

Ford

Amphitheater. On the point is a plaque placed in memory of Ward "Bill" Hall, for whom the trail was named.

Beyond this detour, the Bill Hall Trail begins a moderate ascent of the hill ahead, passing through a charred woodland of piñon and juniper. After topping the hill at 7,206 feet, the trail angles briefly downhill and then gently ascends the rim to turn south just east of Monument Point. Backpackers en route to Thunder River and Deer Creek will continue following the trail. To reach Monument Point, leave the trail here and walk about 75 yards up to the 7,166-foot point for a rewarding panorama. Fine vistas extend northwest across the vast tableland of the Kanab Plateau to the distant Vermilion Cliffs. Views into the Grand Canyon open up below and to the south. The slickrock expanse of Tapeats Amphitheater spreads out far below, surrounded by Muav Saddle, Powell Plateau, Steamboat Mountain, and Bridgers Knoll. Great Thumb Mesa looms boldly on the South Rim, separated from your vantage point by the 6-mile-wide void of the Grand Canyon.

Your view also stretches far away to the southwest down the trough of the central Grand Canyon. Sheer cliffs of Redwall limestone embrace the deep Inner Gorge. These cliffs are flanked on both sides by the extensive red sandstone platform of The Esplanade. The forested hills of Mounts Logan and Trumbull define the western horizon. After enjoying the memorable vistas, retrace your steps to the trailhead.

Miles and Directions

0.0 Start at the Bill Hall trailhead.

0.8 Arrive at Monument Point; turnaround point.

1.6 Arrive back at the Bill Hall trailhead.

About the Authors

Ron Adkison, an avid hiker and backpacker, began his outdoor explorations at age six. Over his lifetime he logged more than 12,000 trail miles in ten western states. He walked every trail in this guide, most of them multiple times, to provide precise, firsthand information about the trails, as well as features of ecological and historical interest.

Ron shared his love for the backcountry in this guidebook, one of the sixteen he wrote covering wild country in the American West.

After Ron's death in September 2009, his son, Ben Adkison, took over the tasks of revising and updating his books. Ron brought Ben on many of the trips in this book and many others when Ben was young. Ben is now a professional mountain guide and freelance photographer, taking pictures and leading climbs on mountains from Alaska to Antarctica. He also loves to travel, ski, and climb mountains. Ben splits his time between Montana and Alaska. Follow his adventures at www.benadkisonphotography.com.

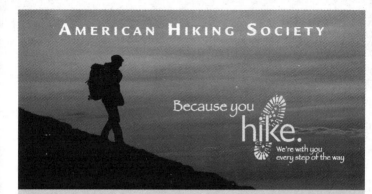

AMERICAN HIKING SOCIETY

Because you hike.
We're with you every step of the way

American Hiking Society gives voice to the more than 75 million Americans who hike and is the only national organization that promotes and protects foot trails, the natural areas that surround them, and the hiking experience. Our work is inspiring and challenging, and is built on three pillars:

Volunteerism and Stewardship
We organize and coordinate nationally recognized programs—including Volunteer Vacations, National Trails Day ®, and the National Trails Fund— that help keep our trails open, safe, and enjoyable.

Policy and Advocacy
We work with Congress and federal agencies to ensure funding for trails, the preservation of natural areas, and the protection of the hiking experience.

Outreach and Education
We expand and support the national constituency of hikers through outreach and education as well as partnerships with other recreation and conservation organizations.

Join us in our efforts. Become an American Hiking Society member today!

American Hiking Society

1422 Fenwick Lane · Silver Spring, MD 20910 · (800) 972-8608
www.AmericanHiking.org · info@AmericanHiking.org